D1466243

The Unions
Structure, Development, and Management

John O. Boonstra

The Unions

Structure, Development, and Management

Marten Estey

University of Pennsylvania

Under the general editorship of

Leonard R. Sayles   *Columbia University*

Harcourt, Brace & World, Inc.

New York / Chicago / San Francisco / Atlanta

ISBN: 0-15-557791-3

Library of Congress Catalog Card Number: 66-25138

Printed in the United States of America

To Mitch

Foreword

As a long-time student of the labor movement, a diligent and respected researcher, and a teacher with a sense of balance and synthesis, Professor Estey was an obvious candidate to write this book. It is never easy to reduce great quantities of knowledge about a subject—particularly one in which the writer excels—to a lean muscular work that embraces all aspects while also providing some of the fat of detail and insight. Professor Estey has indeed done both. He has reduced a substantial body of material to a clear, concise statement, and somehow—and this is the essence of his art—he has managed to ease its terseness with a style and readability that will attract a wide range of readers in and out of the academic world.

If one could have but one book with which to become conversant with the American labor movement, one would be wise to choose this new study by Marten Estey.

Leonard Sayles

Preface

This book was written primarily for the student—whether in college or in business—who wants a brief but analytical account of what unions are, why they behave as they do, and how they are managed, as well as an account of the rules under which they operate.

The primary emphasis is on the nature of unions as organizations and on the similarities and differences between unions and the business organizations with which they deal. Accordingly, the text includes analyses of (1) the patterns of union growth; (2) the evolution of union organizational forms and models in response to changing needs and circumstances; (3) the present organizational structure of the American labor movement and the functions of its components; (4) the business-like versus the democratic aspects of union behavior; and (5) the decision-making process within unions.

Finally, in recognition of the fact that most college students of the current generation were born a full decade after the problem of labor's civil rights was as burning a public issue as the civil rights of minorities is today, a chapter is devoted to the historic development of the law with respect to unions.

If this analysis substitutes light for some of the heat which readers of all persuasions are apt to bring to the subject, it will have served its purpose.

Marten Estey

Contents

Foreword   vii

Preface   ix

1   The Changing Dimensions of the Labor Movement   1

2   Evolving Union Models: A Brief History   12

3   Anatomy of the Labor Movement   35

4   The Management of Unions   46

5   The Behavior of Unions   72

6   The State and the Unions   92

Epilogue: The Future of Unionism   117

Index   119

The Unions
Structure, Development, and Management

The Changing Dimensions of the Labor Movement

The American labor movement (a collective term for labor unions with headquarters in the United States) is a complex institution, the culmination of over 150 years of activity, of expansion and regression, of ebb and flow. It is the resultant of a myriad of economic and social forces, personal influences, and chance events. Like other social institutions, it is no monolith, but is composed of vastly varied components ranging from the minuscule to the gigantic, from the young to the old, from the expanding to the declining.

Total Membership

In 1964, the most recent date for which we have detailed statistics, American unions claimed a total of nearly 18.5 million members.[1] Some 1.25 million of

[1] United States Department of Labor, Bureau of Labor Statistics, *Directory of National and International Unions in the United States, 1965,* Bulletin No. 1493 (Washington, D.C.: U.S. Government Printing Office, 1966), p. 49.

Membership of unions with headquarters in the United States was 17,975,532, not counting approximately 452,000 members of local independent unions in the United States. Taken together, the combined total is 18,427,532, of whom 1,240,000 were outside the United States. Total union membership in the United States was 17,187,532.

Unless otherwise indicated, all union membership data in this chapter are from this source, or from unpublished BLS figures.

them were outside the United States (principally in Canada), so that in the United States alone there were over 17 million union members. These 17 million union members represented about 22 per cent of the total United States labor force and 30 per cent of all employees in nonagricultural establishments. Because figures on employment in nonagricultural establishments include a substantial number of executives and managers who are not eligible for union membership, it is probably accurate to say that the number of union members in the United States is now equal to one-third of those eligible to join.

Membership Trends

To put these figures into meaningful perspective, let us look briefly at the trends they reflect. Unionism of the size and scale we know today is a fairly recent phenomenon, for although unions appeared in the United States before 1800, total membership in 1900 was still less than one million. Not until 1937 did union membership permanently pass the 5 million mark, and only since 1950 has total membership been consistently above the 15 million level. What might properly be called the present labor movement, in fact, may be said to have started in 1933.

In that year, things looked black indeed for the labor movement. Union membership had dropped below 3 million, to the lowest level in seventeen years; only one of every nine employees in nonagricultural establishments, and only one of every twenty men in the labor force as a whole, belonged to a union. So grim was the outlook, in fact, that Professor George E. Barnett, a distinguished labor economist and historian, in his presidential address to the American Economic Association, prophesied: "I see no reason to believe that American trade unionism will so revolutionize itself within a short period of time as to become in the next decade a more potent social influence than it has been in the past decade."[2]

In fact, however, 1933 proved an historic turning point for organized labor. Starting in that year, total union membership, spurred first by New Deal labor legislation and then by World War II, underwent an expansion unprecedented in both amount and duration, more than quadrupling in the decade 1933–1944 and continuing with only an occasional interruption until 1956, when it reached an all-time high of 18,477,000, a figure more than six times that of 1933. Meanwhile, the proportion of union members had risen to include one of every three employees in nonagricultural establishments and one in four of the over-all labor force.

Immediately following this peak, union membership fell into a five-year decline, so that between 1956 and 1961 total membership dropped by more

[2] George E. Barnett, "American Trade Unionism and Social Insurance," *American Economic Review*, Vol. XXIII (March 1933), p. 6.

than one million. From 1961 to 1964, under the expansive influence of rising output and employment, the trend was reversed again and over half the loss of the preceding five years recovered. But despite this recovery (which appears to have continued through 1965, when employment rose another 1.8 million and the Auto Workers and the Teamsters alone added over 200,000 members), the inescapable facts are that in 1964 total American union membership was still nearly half a million less than it had been eight years earlier and that nearly a decade had passed since union membership had reached its peak.[3] Not since the doldrums of the 1920's has there been such a protracted slump in union membership.

Relation of Membership Trends to Labor Force Trends

Even more discouraging to union leaders are the recent trends in the *relative* importance of unions, as reflected in the ratio of union membership to the total labor force, or to the number of employees in nonagricultural establishments, a somewhat more relevant figure since unions have no role in the armed services and—at least until recently—very little in agriculture. For although union membership turned down after 1956, the labor force (i.e., the number of workers in the labor market) continued to rise at a vigorous pace. Accordingly, by 1964 the percentage of union members in the total labor force had fallen to its lowest level since 1945 and the percentage of union members in nonagricultural establishments to its lowest point since 1942.

In fact, given the projected expansion of the labor force to 86 million by 1970,[4] American unions would have to gain nearly two million additional members in the United States alone—an expansion of more than ten per cent —just to maintain their present share of the total U.S. labor force and to avoid further deterioration of their position.

Equally crucial for organized labor has been the fact that in the past ten or fifteen years the labor force has not only expanded, but changed internally, and in a way generally unfavorable to unions, with continuing shifts from the most unionized industries and occupations to those in which unions have so far been least successful.

Shift to White-collar Occupations

Whether or not there was a cause and effect relationship between the two events, it is at least symbolic that the downturn of union membership from its peak should have occurred in 1956, when, for the first time, the number

---

[3] If we exclude some 452,000 members of local independent unions, first reported in 1962.

[4] *Manpower Report of the President* (Washington, D.C.: U.S. Government Printing Office, March 1966), p. 37.

of white-collar workers (25.6 million) rose above the number of blue-collar workers (25.2 million), who were and still are the base on which the labor movement is built, and who for generations were the largest group in the labor force as well. The shift to white-collar work by no means ceased when this milestone was passed, for, by June 1965, the spread had increased to 5 million, with 32 million white-collar workers as against 27 million in blue-collar jobs. *This* is where organized labor has felt the pinch. And just how sharp this pinch is may be suggested by the report that between 1956 and 1964 *union membership* among white-collar workers showed a net gain of only 122,000, while simultaneously the *number* of white-collar workers rose by five million.

So far as union growth prospects are concerned, the adverse impact of the long-run shift of workers out of blue-collar and into white-collar jobs is reinforced by two other closely related developments—the long-run shift in employment from the goods-producing industries to the service industries and the continuous rise in the proportion of women in the labor force.

Shift from Goods-producing to Service Industries

Until about 1950, the production industries had provided the bulk of the employment in the economy. Then, for the first time, the number of workers in the service industries—wholesale and retail trade; federal, state, and local government; transportation and public utilities; finance, insurance, and real estate; and others—overtook the number employed in the production industries—manufacturing, construction, mining, agriculture. By May 1966, employment in the service industries had grown to some 40.2 million out of 63.0 million employees on nonagricultural payrolls, or 63 per cent of the total, while employment in production industries had dropped to 37 per cent of the total.

Behind these shifts in the composition of the labor force lies another economic factor—technological change and rising productivity. Whether we call it automation or not is immaterial; the fact is that rising productivity in the production industries has made it possible to produce more goods with the same number of workers, or even more goods with fewer workers. Accordingly, output has risen without a corresponding rise in employment or in union membership in the production industries. Rising output has also increased the need for labor in the distributive and service industries and thus has augmented the shift of employment from the production to the service industries.

Increased Employment of Women

Technological change also has increased the efficiency with which the housewife performs her domestic chores and has released her for outside employment at a time when employment opportunities are expanding in white-collar and service industry occupations, which are generally more suited to women's tastes and training than production or blue-collar jobs. As a result, the percentage of women in the labor force has been rising slowly but steadily—from 20 per cent in 1920 to 32 per cent in 1960. It is expected that by 1970 women will comprise 34 per cent of the labor force.

Each of these shifts in the internal composition of the labor force poses a problem for the unions, for each represents a move from a group among which unions have been most successful—male, blue-collar, production workers—to a group in which unions have made the least headway—female, white-collar, service employees. And since labor force projections for the next fifteen to twenty years indicate that these shifts will continue, the prospects do not seem bright for an early reversal of the decline in the *relative* importance of unions in the labor force.

The decline in actual union membership, coinciding with a rise in the labor force concentrated in those industries and occupations that unions have found hardest to organize, has become the basis for gloomy references to stagnation and decline of the labor movement.

Long-Run Membership Growth

A look at the long-run growth of union membership, however, may provide a more dispassionate standard by which to evaluate the situation. It shows clearly that an expansion such as took place in the period 1933 to 1956 is the exception rather than the rule. The American labor movement has never grown steadily and evenly; its greatest gains have come in spurts, during which unions have made significant and usually lasting breakthroughs into new territory.

Thus, in the sixty-eight years from 1897 to 1964 (the period for which we have annual statistics of union membership), total union membership grew from a scant 447,000 to over 18 million members, for a net gain of close to 18 million. The bulk of this growth has been concentrated into five short periods when membership rose both rapidly and substantially, as shown below:[5]

Years	Net Gain
1897–1904	1,625,700
1915–1920	2,465,200
1933–1939	3,582,500
1940–1944	5,346,000
1949–1953	2,620,700

[5] Data used here are from Leo Troy, *Trade Union Membership, 1897–1962*, Occasional Paper 92 (New York: National Bureau of Economic Research, 1965), p. 1.

While the precise dates of these periods and the amounts of change that occurred during them is the subject of scholarly debate, the fact remains that a combined gain of 16,445,000 members, or an amount equivalent to nearly 90 per cent of the over-all gain for the whole period, was concentrated in just twenty-seven of the sixty-eight years.

These figures also illustrate dramatically the impact of war on union membership, for they show that three times since 1900, wartime economic conditions have been a stimulus to union growth—during World War I, World War II, and the Korean War. The war in Vietnam undoubtedly has had similar effect. In fact, there have been only two periods of notable membership growth that lacked the stimulus of war—1897–1904 and 1933–1939 (the New Deal period).

Thus, it is not the present lack of growth of membership that is unprecedented, but rather the virtually uninterrupted expansion of membership from 1933 to 1956. Unions may now be returning to what has been, historically, their normal status. Needless to say, such an analysis provides only cold comfort for union leaders who, like other managers, prefer expansion and growth to stability or decline.

Individual Union Membership Changes

The current picture of the labor movement is not *entirely* dismal, however, for the rise and fall of membership of the labor movement as a whole does not reflect similar rises and falls for each national union; instead, the over-all pattern is a composite of divergent trends, the net result of a variety of movements. Even during the sharpest declines in total union membership, some unions will expand and grow; even the most exuberant periods of over-all growth are not shared by all unions.

Indeed, since each union operates in an economic and social environment which differs from that of any other union (in some cases only slightly, in others very significantly), it is understandable that no two unions would find economic conditions alike; no two unions would face the same combination of stimulating or retarding influences.

There is no more dramatic evidence of the great differences in union fortunes that can occur simultaneously than that offered by a comparison of the Teamsters Union and the United Mine Workers in the period 1951–1964. During this time, the leading growth union, by a wide margin, was the Teamsters Union which, having moved from less than 100,000 members in 1933 to one million in 1951, continued its spectacular growth (though at a somewhat slower rate) to over 1.5 million in 1964. This gain of more than 50 per cent between 1951 and 1964 moved the union from the rank of third largest to that of the largest in the country.

Meanwhile, the United Mine Workers of America which, beginning in

1898, was for all but four out of 44 consecutive years the largest union in the United States, and in 1951 was still ranked sixth largest, declined—as a direct result of drastic and lasting reductions in employment in the coal industry—from 600,000 members in 1951 to an estimated 150,000 in 1964, a loss of 75 per cent of its peak membership!

Available evidence indicates that such diversity, while not generally as dramatic as this, is widespread in the labor movement. According to the most recent BLS study, in the period 1951–1964 the number of unions reporting membership gains (61) was nearly equaled by the number reporting losses (60).

But such data, useful as they are in demonstrating that the over-all picture conceals widely varying experiences, fail to reveal what is perhaps the most significant and meaningful information of all—the *identity* of the leading unions in both the growth and decline stages.

Of the fifteen largest individual unions, which together account for more than half the total membership of the American labor movement, eight made a net gain in membership between 1956 and 1964, while seven suffered a decline. The unions that grew during this period and their net gains are as follows:

Teamsters	139,000
Electrical Workers (IBEW)	131,000
Retail Clerks	128,000
Operating Engineers	111,000
Building Service Employees	90,000
Communications Workers	35,000
Meat Cutters	34,000
Hotel Employees	3,500

Membership losses were distributed as follows:

Auto Workers	152,000
Machinists	142,000
Carpenters	90,000
Steelworkers	39,000
Laborers	34,000
Ladies Garment Workers	8,000
Amalgamated Clothing Workers	8,000

Even a cursory inspection of these two lists reveals the significant fact that membership gains are concentrated among unions in the service industries, while losses are concentrated among unions in the manufacturing industries.

Equally important, taking the group as a whole, is the fact that gains exceeded losses by 225,000 members—668,000 gained to 443,000 lost.

Do these figures indicate a greater ability on the part of American unions to cope with the changing composition of the labor force than is generally recognized?

The Distribution of Union Membership

Industrial Distribution

Just as the industrial composition of the labor force changes, so the industrial composition of the labor movement is undergoing gradual but continuous change.

Changes of this sort have been evident ever since detailed statistics of membership for individual unions became available. In the first quarter of the twentieth century, the core of union strength was to be found in the railroad and the building trades unions, which together accounted for 42 per cent of total membership in 1903 and 47 per cent in 1923. This situation changed permanently during the 1930's, in part because of the rise of the CIO, and in part because of the change of the composition of industry itself. In 1939, for example, while the Mine Workers were still the largest single union and the building trades included three of the fifteen largest unions, no railroad union was among the ten largest, having been replaced by unions in the manufacturing industries—namely, Auto Workers, Steelworkers, and two clothing workers' unions.

Between 1951 and 1964 the picture was shifting again, with membership in railroad, mining, textile, communications, transportation equipment, and metalworking industries declining, while expansion was taking place in government service, printing, retail trade, construction, and trucking. And in the expansion between 1962 and 1964, while membership in manufacturing industries rose by about 300,000 as a result of both the war in Vietnam and the generally high levels of economic activity, membership among government employees rose by some 228,000, so that government employees, who in 1956 had accounted for only 5.1 per cent of all union members, now represented 8.1 per cent of the total.

Nevertheless, the stronghold of unions in the old established areas is not readily broken; in 1964, three major industry groups—metals and machinery, transportation, and construction—still accounted for more than 40 per cent of all union members. The continued importance of transportation as a center of union activity is now due, of course, to the presence of the Teamsters rather than to a resurgence of the railroad unions.

White-Collar Membership

Data on the number and distribution of white-collar union members is limited and has been available only since 1956. In that year it was estimated that 2,463,000 white-collar workers belonged to American unions and that they represented approximately 13.6 per cent of total membership. During the slump in union membership from 1956 to 1961, white-collar membership fell off more than proportionately, so that by 1960 they represented only 12.2

per cent of over-all membership. Since 1960, white-collar membership has risen by nearly 400,000, and their share of total membership has risen to its highest point, 14.4 per cent. White-collar membership is smallest in manufacturing industries (about 328,000) and greatest in nonmanufacturing industries (about 1.6 million); about 636,000 (25 per cent) of all white-collar members are in government service.

Women Members

Women have long been regarded as particularly difficult for unions to organize, and the facts confirm this belief. In 1964, only one of every seven women in the labor force was a union member as compared to one in every four men.

The female contingent in the labor movement tends to be concentrated in certain industries and certain unions. Thus, the 353,900 women in the International Ladies' Garment Workers' Union and the 282,800 in the Amalgamated Clothing Workers make up not only over 75 per cent of the membership of each of these two unions, but nearly 20 per cent of all women union members as well. Add to these figures the women belonging to the Electrical Workers, the Retail Clerks, and the Hotel Employees—each of which claims over 200,000 women members—and we find that these five unions together account for nearly 40 per cent of the total female union membership.

On the other hand, one-quarter of all national unions report no women members, while in another quarter women represent less than 10 per cent of the membership. It will be interesting to see whether this pattern is affected by the Civil Rights Act of 1964 which, among other things, makes it unlawful for unions to "exclude or expel from its membership, or otherwise to discriminate against any individual because of his race, color, religion, sex, or national origin."

Geographic Distribution

Long-run shifts in the industrial and occupational composition of the labor force, however, have not changed the fact that the labor movement in the United States is a predominantly urban phenomenon.

Accordingly, in 1964, five states had more than a million union members each—New York (2.5 million), California (1.9 million), Pennsylvania (1.4 million), Illinois (1.4 million), and Ohio (1.1 million). Together these five states accounted for 8,387,000 union members, or approximately half of total United States membership. And union membership in these states averaged 37 per cent of the employees in nonagricultural establishments as against the United States average of 29.5 per cent.

At the other extreme are five states with less than 25,000 union members each—South Dakota (14,000), Wyoming (19,000), North Dakota (21,000), Alaska (21,000), and Vermont (22,000). These five states had a combined membership of only 97,000, which represented only 19.0 per cent of their nonagricultural employees and less than one per cent of total United States membership. Relatively speaking, however, the least unionized state was North Carolina, whose 89,000 union members represented only 6.7 per cent of its nonagricultural labor force.

The geographic centers of union membership are also shifting, following the persistent westward movement of population and industry. In 1939, the five states with the largest union membership were New York, Pennsylvania, Illinois, Ohio, and California, in that order. Twenty-five years later, California had risen from fifth to second place as a result of a more than fourfold increase in membership, while both Pennsylvania and Ohio slipped back one rank because of a decline in membership between 1953 and 1964.

The Frontier Unions

In addition to unions such as the Teamsters, the Electrical Workers, and the Clerks, which might reasonably be labeled "growth unions," on the grounds that they are the chief sources of membership gains, there are other unions which, although their gains are numerically small, are important because they are on the frontier of union activity. They are where the venture capital of labor is being invested.

In some cases, the "frontier" unions are themselves new creations, having developed from scratch to fill an institutional vacuum. In this category is the National Farm Workers Association, formed in 1962. In 1965, in conjunction with the Agricultural Workers Organizing Committee, AFL-CIO, it waged an eight-month strike of grape-pickers in Delano, California, which resulted in the Schenley Corporation agreeing to allow the union to represent its farm laborers. In September 1966, the two organizations merged to form the United Farm Workers Organizing Committee, AFL-CIO and won the right to represent grape-pickers at two of the DiGiorgio Corporation ranches.[6]

What was noteworthy about the unionization of grape-pickers was that it was virtually the first successful attempt at collective action and unionization among migratory farm laborers, a group which, despite employment conditions that are far below modern industrial standards (lacking even the protection of most of the social and labor legislation of the past thirty years), has been so transient and shifting that it has long been regarded as unorganizable.

Another example of union penetration of new territory is provided by the achievements in the past five years of teachers' unions. Teachers' unions, in

[6] *The New York Times,* September 3, 1966.

contrast to the Farm Workers, are old and well established; the American Federation of Teachers, for example, was founded in 1916. As recently as 1960, it claimed only 56,000 members, but between 1961 and 1964 teachers' strikes on an unprecedented scale won them substantial economic gains in New York City and elsewhere; a new militancy was demonstrated and, by 1964, the AFTE reported a membership of 100,000—a gain in four years of nearly 100 per cent.

The past several years have also seen a flurry of activity in private, non-profit institutions, most notably hospitals. There is no national union for hospital employees as such; instead, organizing activities and campaigns have been undertaken by unions that have, for one reason or another, chosen to take a special interest in hospital employees. In New York City, the spear-head of hospital-organizing activities has been a union whose membership is primarily in the retail drug store field—Local 1199, Retail, Wholesale and Department Store Union. In other cases, unions of laundry workers, of cafeteria employees, and of building service employees have conducted organizing drives among their counterparts in hospitals.

Union activities in the medical field have also been extended to members of the professional staff. In New York City, public health nurses successfully struck for higher salaries in May 1966,[7] and doctors employed by the city Health Department won salary increases and other gains after a week-long work stoppage in June 1966.[8]

Nor have the arts remained immune to the ferment of union activity. Dancers of the American Ballet Theater recently won gains by threatening to strike,[9] and, in 1966, the Philadelphia Orchestra struck for eight weeks.

But perhaps the most novel manifestation of union activity was the formation, in October 1966, of the American Federation of Priests, under the leadership of Father DuBay, a Catholic priest suspended for outspoken support of the civil rights movement.[10]

Again, here in a nutshell is the problem of the labor movement: Most of its largest unions have been concentrated in the production industries, in which membership is contracting because employment is declining, while growth is primarily in the service industries, where unions are generally smaller. The extent of this growth has thus far been modest in absolute terms. On the other hand, the fact that the growth sectors of the labor movement coincide so closely with the growth sectors of the labor force suggests that unions may be adapting somewhat more effectively to the changing environment than is generally recognized, even though growth in these areas is not yet sufficiently vigorous to compensate for losses elsewhere.

[7] *Ibid.*, May 30, 1966.
[8] *Ibid.*, June 30, 1966.
[9] *Ibid.*, September 2, 1966.
[10] *Ibid.*, October 20, 1966.

2

Evolving Union Models:
A Brief History

The stream of events which make up the history of the American labor movement can be viewed from a number of perspectives. Each is accurate and meaningful, but each is necessarily selective; none can reveal the whole story.

Here we view labor history as a series of conflicts and experiments in organizational theory. Omitting the drama of famous strikes and lockouts and the historic developments in the substantive terms of employment, we concentrate on the no less significant history of labor's search for the organizational models and programs best suited to the needs and objectives of the members and for survival in the American economic and social environment.

The Beginnings

The development of labor organization in the United States is no recent phenomenon; in fact, the appearance of permanent labor unions, roughly comparable to those we know now, occurred nearly 175 years ago, at the end of the eighteenth century: shoemakers organized in Philadelphia in 1792, carpenters in Boston in 1793, and printers in New York in 1794.[1]

[1] The information in this section is drawn largely from two excellent histories of the labor movement: Harry A. Millis and Royal E. Montgomery, *The Economics of Labor,* Vol. III, *Organized Labor* (New York: McGraw-Hill, 1945), pp. 12–73; and Joseph G. Rayback, *A History of American Labor* (New York: Free Press, 1966), pp. 54–184.

These first unions were unions of craftsmen, who possessed both the motivation for organization and the bargaining power to make unions effective. But the bargaining techniques of these early unions were rather primitive by today's standards, for give and take bargaining and compromise, the essence of bargaining as we know it, were largely unknown. If a union struck for higher wages or a closed shop it was usually on an all or nothing basis—the workers either got their full demands or they got nothing; and more often than not it was nothing. The concept of compromise and negotiation did not develop in practice until after the Civil War. But otherwise, the economic orientation of these early unions was clear enough—they were the unmistakable forerunners of today's business unions.

Organizationally speaking, their chief problem was their great vulnerability to economic recession. Repeatedly, they made real headway during periods of economic expansion and boom. And just as repeatedly, during periods of recession, many—perhaps the majority—simply disintegrated and disappeared. Most of the unions formed in the expansion of 1834–1836, for instance, were wiped out by the panic of 1837, and such major economic slides as those of 1857 and 1873 had similar repercussions.

During these recessions, when the economically oriented trade unions were either disbanded or totally ineffective, workers sought other methods of improving their position; many switched to political activity or joined the ranks of the various reform movements. Labor's first political party, for example, came into existence in 1828 in the midst of a recession, when the Mechanics' Union of Philadelphia was transformed into the Republican Political Association of the Workingmen of Philadelphia; the following year a Working Men's Party was formed in New York City.

Following the panic of 1837, in particular, the uplift and humanitarian sentiments were very strong, and programs ranging from utopian socialism (such as that of the Owenite communities based on the New Harmony experiment) to producers' cooperatives and land reform absorbed much of labor's organizational energies. But, with the return of prosperity, political action and social reform lost their appeal as workers became more interested in the immediate goals of higher wages and better working conditions, and unions were revived or reorganized and the whole cycle began again.

While it vastly oversimplifies the developments on the labor scene between 1800 and 1885, it is fair to say that this dichotomy between political action and economic activity characterized much of the period. Labor vacillated between the two approaches, trying them in different forms and combinations and constantly seeking to strike the proper balance—to find an organizational model and a program which would be the most effective answer to their needs.

Meanwhile, however, the labor movement was gradually developing into something more than just a scattering of isolated and independent local craft unions. Its structure grew vertically as well as horizontally. And, in fact, by 1837, industrial unions as well as craft unions,[2] national unions, and labor federations—almost all the structural forms later developed at one time or another—had made their initial appearance.

In 1827, as part of their drive to secure the ten-hour day in Philadelphia, some fifteen unions formed the Mechanics' Union of Trade Associations— the first city-wide federation of labor unions. By 1836, city federations could be found in some thirteen cities, including most of the major cities on the eastern seaboard.

In 1831, the New England Association of Farmers, Mechanics, and Other Workmen was formed in Providence to organize not just skilled workers but factory operatives as well; basically, it was an early forerunner of industrial unionism—over a century before the founding of the CIO.

Unions in various occupations began to organize along national lines to control competition between unions in different cities. Carpenters, shoe-makers, comb-makers, hand-loom weavers, and printers all created national organizations in the period 1834–1837—and all collapsed and disappeared during the depression of 1837.

Even a preliminary attempt at a federation of craft unions was made during this period with the establishment of the National Trades' Union in 1834, the "first federated body in the United States attempting to bring within its membership all local unions, nationals, and city centrals."[3] Like the national unions, this early federation was wiped out in the depression of 1837. But the groundwork had been laid; the seeds of all later organizational forms had been sown.

Beginning shortly before the Civil War, national organizations of craft unions became increasingly numerous and, more important, sufficiently durable for the first time to survive recession. By the end of the 1860's, some thirty national craft unions were active, many of which were to be instrumental in the eventual establishment of the American Federation of Labor.

In 1866, the National Labor Union, a national federation embracing both craft unionists and reform groups, was organized. Although it lasted only six years before being converted into a political party (a party which subsequently collapsed when its presidential candidate withdrew from the election of 1872), in its short existence the National Labor Union set a record for longevity of a national federation. It was indicative of the growing pressure for a national organization which would serve the common interests of labor in different trades and occupations.

---

[2] Craft unions embrace workers of one skill or occupation; industrial unions, workers in a particular industry or group of industries, regardless of occupation. See Chapter 3, p. 40 for fuller discussion.

[3] Millis and Montgomery, *op. cit.*, p. 32.

The Knights of Labor

By all odds the most successful failure among the labor organizations of the nineteenth century was the Noble Order of the Knights of Labor. Founded in 1871 as a secret society, the Knights came into the open as a national organization in 1878, just as a business boom was beginning.

Although they welcomed craft unions into their midst, the Knights regarded pure and simple craft unionism as tending to separate, rather than unify, the working class; they sought to unite all "real" producers—farmers, lower middle class, and wage earners—into one organization. Structurally, the Knights' basic units, the assemblies, generally brought skilled and unskilled workers together, a fact which proved increasingly distasteful to the craftsmen, if for no other reason than that it interfered with their bargaining effectiveness. And organizationally, the Knights were centralized rather than decentralized, with no provision for national unions; their rules, in fact, prohibited national trade associations. So far as program was concerned, they were opposed in principle to strikes and were more interested in reform and education than in immediate economic gains.

The Knights, in short, were the polar opposite of the craft-union model of organization—indeed, theirs may be considered a primitive model of industrial unionism, without the business-union approach of today's industrial unions.

Both the rise and the fall of the Knights of Labor were spectacular. In 1883, five years after they came into the open, the Knights claimed barely 50,000 members. But in 1884 and 1885 recession struck, and as the unions suffered their customary decline the workers turned "from the empty larder of business unionism to the attractive menu of an uplift association."[4] And when the Knights, successful in spite of themselves, won a strike in 1885 against Jay Gould, at that time "perhaps the most powerful capitalist in the United States,"[5] 600,000 members joined in a single year.

In 1886, at their peak strength, the Knights had nearly 700,000 members —not much by today's standards, but an all-time high at that point in history. Yet, two years later, the Knights' membership had fallen to 220,000, and by 1890, only four years after reaching its apogee, the Knights' membership had dwindled to 100,000 and the fledgling AFL, founded at the peak of the Knights' strength, had already won the allegiance of a majority of the trade unions. The Knights had been a true meteor on the labor horizon—a brilliant flash that burned out.

The sudden disintegration of the Knights was due to a combination of circumstances. Among other things, they had been hurt by the Haymarket riot of May 1886, precipitated when a bomb was thrown at police trying to

[4] *Ibid.*, p. 63.
[5] *Loc. cit.*

disperse a protest meeting against "police brutality" during a strike at the McCormick Reaper plant in Chicago. In the ensuing riot, several persons were fatally wounded and many others injured. Although not implicated in the affair, the Knights undoubtedly suffered from the widespread antilabor sentiment and fear that Haymarket provoked—fear so great that one prominent Chicago businessman, building a new house in 1890, installed a button marked "MOB" which he could punch to call the police.[6] Without a business union base to fall back on, the Knights were harder hit than their competitor, the AFL.

The American Federation of Labor and Craft Unionism

One of the key elements in the decline and fall of the Knights was the appearance of the American Federation of Labor, which, when founded in 1886, benefited substantially from the dissatisfaction of the craft unions with the "one big union" approach and the consequent failure of the Knights to give greater attention to their particular needs.

The AFL,[7] in fact, was both a response and a reaction to the Knights of Labor: a response in that it was organized precisely when the discontent of the craft unionists offered a golden opportunity for an organization designed to meet their needs; and a reaction in that the phenomenal growth of the Knights, especially in 1886, had been partly at the expense of the existing craft unions. The Knights had not been hesitant to raid the craft unions, and the formation of the AFL may be seen in part as a defensive measure by the craft unions.

As we examine the structure and policies of the AFL (the most successful of their kind thus far devised), it should be emphasized that they were not simply the result of a stroke of inspired genius on the part of Samuel Gompers and his fellow union leaders in the AFL. Rather, it should be clear that the structure and policies of the AFL were the fruit of over fifty years of trial and error in the American labor movement—Gompers and company knew well the lessons of those fifty years experience and applied them in creating the new federation.

A word about Gompers is in order, nevertheless. Chosen first president of the American Federation of Labor in 1886 at the age of 36, Gompers remained president until 1924 with only one interruption—in 1894, when he was out of office for a year after a close defeat at the convention.

Gompers came to the AFL from the Cigar Makers Union and, needless to say, was a staunch defender of the craft-union point of view. It has been suggested that the chief reason he was chosen to head the AFL was that no

---

[6] Irving Bernstein, "Union Growth and Structural Cycles," *Proceedings,* Industrial Relations Research Association, 1954, p. 205 n.

[7] For many generations, the letters "AFL" (or "A. F. of L.," as it called itself) referred, not to a football league, but to the American Federation of Labor, a union league, as it were.

full-time union leader would accept the post in an organization so lacking in promise as the young AFL.[8] Yet, when he died four decades later, Gompers had left an indelible mark, not only on the AFL, but on the labor movement as a whole. Gompers' genius, as we have suggested, lay not in his ability to invent new approaches and policies, but rather in his understanding of the strengths and weaknesses of the Federation and in his skill in making the most of them.

The founding of the American Federation of Labor in 1886 not only falls at the midpoint between the first American labor case in 1806 and this writing (1966), but in a very real sense it marks the beginning of modern unionism as we know it today.

Like others before it, the AFL represented a particular model of unionism —craft unionism—and it offered this model as an alternative and an improvement upon models that had gone before. It expected its craft federation model to correct some of the shortcomings of previous models and to provide an adequate solution to problems which previous models had found insurmountable.

In retrospect, we can say that a notable feature of the craft-union model of labor organization, as pursued and practiced by the AFL and its affiliated national unions, was that it was the first to survive the rigors of business fluctuations without simply disintegrating and having to start over. In short, the AFL model was the first to achieve permanence, regardless of economic conditions. Indeed, while it had many other shortcomings, as we will see subsequently, the AFL maintained an unbroken and continuous existence for nearly seventy years, from 1886 until its merger with the CIO in 1955. This alone gives the AFL a unique place in American labor history.

It seems quite likely that it was skillful management as much as the inherent advantages of craft unionism that accounted for the great success of the craft-union model in the hands of the AFL.

The basic policies—the managerial formula, as it were—for the administration of the AFL, as enunciated by Samuel Gompers, its first president, and adhered to with little variation until the rise of the CIO forced a change, were clearly defined. Central to Gompers' administrative formula were two basic policies: first, that the national unions which belonged to the AFL were to be guaranteed "trade autonomy"; and second, that they were to be afforded "exclusive jurisdiction" over their particular craft or occupation.

To use modern business terminology, the promise of "trade autonomy" meant that decision-making was to be decentralized, with the national unions retaining the ultimate authority to make decisions for themselves. Although it applied to all activities of the national unions, economic and political alike, this decentralization was particularly important when it came to the unions' main function, collective bargaining, for it meant (among other things) that,

[8] Philip Taft, *The A. F. of L. in the Time of Gompers* (New York: Harper & Row, 1957), p. 39.

on the union side, collective-bargaining decisions would be made by those best equipped by knowledge and experience to know the problems involved —the officers of the union in the occupation or trade—rather than by some general officer from the Federation offices in Washington.

Similarly, the policy of exclusive jurisdiction was the labor union counterpart of the exclusive business franchise or dealership. By granting the Carpenters Union, for example, exclusive jurisdiction in its field, the AFL recognized its sole authority to organize carpenters (and the sole right of members of the Carpenters Union to do "carpenters' work"). Thus, it was protected against possible competition from other unions by assurances that no other unions would be given overlapping jurisdiction, and no competitor (if they already existed) would be recognized by the AFL. That this policy proved to be harder to administer and enforce than to enunciate was not entirely the fault of Gompers or the AFL; the problem, as we shall see later, was that changing technology kept upsetting the neat divisions of power that the AFL laid out, forcing the constant re-examination of the question of jurisdiction over occupations and jobs that had not existed when the original charters were issued.

Taken together, the policies of autonomy and exclusive jurisdiction proved remarkably successful in attracting organizations to the new federation, and it is not hard to understand—they gave the national unions a great deal of freedom.

Autonomy insured their freedom from intervention by the Federation. It should be emphasized, of course, that it was not a question of the Federation offering the national unions a new and attractive advantage. The AFL did not *confer* autonomy on the national unions; the plain fact was that the national unions *had* autonomy; they were already independent decision-making organizations. The Federation's strategy was simply to *recognize* their autonomy, realizing that the only way national unions could be induced to join the Federation was by the pledge of hard and fast constitutional guarantees that their independence and autonomy would not be abridged. The AFL was in the position of the United Nations in its early years—trying to attract membership with assurances that sovereignty would not be impaired by joining it.

Exclusive jurisdiction, by giving a national union monopolistic rights to represent the workers in a particular occupation, gave it a measure of freedom from competition from other national unions (whose predatory instincts had been revealed on many occasions). One disadvantage, which at the time of the founding of the AFL might well have seemed remote, was that while exclusive jurisdiction fenced competing unions *out,* it also fenced its possessor *in* and limited its activities to a specific area or occupation.[9] At

9 For an analysis of this point, see Marten S. Estey, "Trends in Concentration of Union Membership, 1897–1962," *Quarterly Journal of Economics,* Vol. LXXX (August 1966), pp. 354–355.

any rate, at the time, the benefits appeared to outweigh the costs. The national unions retained their independence in handling the key union function of collective bargaining and gained protection against competition.

A third key point in the AFL formula was insistence on organization by crafts or trades—the organization of skilled workers, with a separate union for each separate skill or occupational specialty. Economically speaking, the distinctive characteristic of a "skill" is that it is the product of relatively long training. The skilled craftsmen are thus specialists who tend to be both in relatively short supply and, because of their ability, difficult to replace. To be blunt about it, the fact that they are hard to replace gives them great leverage in making demands on their employers; this was and is the prime source of their bargaining power.

In addition, however, the economic power inherent in their skill was enhanced by the organizational structure adopted by the AFL. Establishing a separate union for each district craft or skill—the carpenters, the bricklayers, or the plumbers, for example—gave the workers the advantages of *organizational* as well as *individual* specialization. And because all the members of a single craft union shared a common skill, the problem of formulating union demands was simplified—conflicts of interest *within* the union tended to be minimized and *internal* bargaining in the formulation of union demands was reduced. But undoubtedly the most important advantage of such organizational specialization was that it enabled the unions to focus sharply their economic power so as to bring the greatest possible pressure upon the employers. As Chamberlain has pointed out: "One advantage of the craft union structure is the key position which skilled workers frequently play in an enterprise, coupled with the relatively low wage bill which they entail. A strike of a handful of powerhouse employees may close down an entire plant, involving the employer in a substantial cost of disagreeing on their terms, whereas because of their small number the cost of agreement may be negligible in comparison, even if they demand an 'outrageous' pay increase."[10]

Once the Federation chose to emphasize economic rather than political or other objectives, the craft-union structure was the logical one, for in the economic environment of the late nineteenth century, it was clearly the way to maximize economic gains.

Since the bargaining power of the craft union appeared to be the mechanism through which economic gains could be maximized, it was only sound management to concentrate the unions' limited resources there, where they would do most good. Accordingly, it was an integral part of the AFL formula to emphasize collective bargaining as the primary union function and to give it top priority as the means for achieving union objectives.

The priority given to collective bargaining, of course, had a number of

[10] Neil W. Chamberlain and James W. Kuhn, *Collective Bargaining,* 2nd ed. (New York: McGraw-Hill, 1965), p. 174.

consequences. It meant, in the first place, minimizing the efforts devoted to political activity. It meant a long-run shift of power from the local union to the national union. Most significant of all, it meant that the AFL had chosen business unionism and the path of accommodation and compromise with management.

Closely related to the preceding principles was the AFL view of the role of unions in politics. The craft (or trade[11]) union majority in the Federation, adhering to a philosophy that had been expressed as early as 1872, insisted that the AFL should maintain a nonpartisan political stance, avoiding either entangling alliances with existing political parties or "independent" political action in the form of a separate labor party.

This opposition to partisan political commitment reflected a variety of factors: (1) the conviction that the labor movement should concentrate its energies on collective bargaining and not risk dissipating them in political activity as the Knights of Labor had; (2) a long-standing craft union fear that political ties were more likely to divide than to unify the labor movement, for though workers might be united in their concern for economic improvement at work, it was apparent that on political issues their interests and loyalties were as diverse as those of any other segment of the population; and (3) a realistic recognition that a uniform, Federation-wide political stand, which a partisan political position would imply, was not compatible with the policy of national union autonomy upon which the whole administration of the Federation may be said to have been based.

But its opposition to *partisan* politics did not mean that the Federation sought to remain aloof from politics. Far from it; from the outset, Gompers and his fellow trade-unionists saw that certain problems demanded legislative solutions. The AFL, accordingly, lobbied for specific legislation as needed and adopted the policy of "reward your friends and punish your enemies." This meant that political judgments should be based on the candidates and, more specifically, on their record in matters of labor interest, rather than on their party labels. This technique had the particular advantage, furthermore, of enhancing labor's political bargaining power.

In short, the AFL under Gompers' leadership was not apolitical; it simply chose pressure-group politics in preference to party politics, using its political power to serve its immediate self-interest, as is the usual practice of economic interest groups. Unlike many pressure groups, however, the AFL preferred to put primary reliance upon economic activity for achieving its objectives and to relegate political activity to second place.

Somewhat paradoxically, perhaps, Gompers also advocated what was known in labor circles as "voluntarism," opposing government intervention to improve living or working standards directly by legislation on the grounds that if such benefits were provided by the government, it would interfere with

---

[11] In present-day usage, the two terms are interchangeable.

the unions' role as the source of such gains, and the workers would therefore be less likely to join unions for self-improvement. On these grounds, Gompers found himself in league with employers in opposing government intervention into labor problems.

All in all, Gompers' formula for administering the AFL was remarkably business-like. It recognized the practical values of monopoly (exclusive juris-diction) and of specialization (separate unions for each craft); it concen-trated on decision-making at the plant level or the firm level and opposed centralized decision-making or standard-setting by government. It is no accident that the AFL is identified with the concept of business unionism.

Taken together, these policies proved remarkably successful in attracting unions and members into the new federation. From 1897 to 1904, for ex-ample, when union membership rose even more rapidly than in the expansion of the late 1930's, AFL unions accounted for 1,400,000 new members, or 85 per cent of the 1,625,700 increase in total union membership.[12]

Even more indicative of the young AFL's organizational vigor is the fact that between 1897 and 1904 it issued a total of 92 charters, with the result that the number of its affiliated unions more than doubled, rising to a total of 120 in 1904. This figure was not surpassed for over fifty years, until the AFL-CIO merger in 1955. By 1904, 85 per cent of all national unions in the United States were affiliated with the AFL.[13]

After 1904, growth was less dramatic. By 1914, AFL membership had just passed the 2-million mark. Rising briefly to 4 million, AFL strength, like that of other unions, then declined gradually throughout the 1920's and by 1933 had fallen back to less than 2.5 million.

Nor has the craft-union model lost its validity today. Despite the vast changes in the industrial environment and in technology, and the structural upheaval in organized labor in the 1930's, the craft unions are still a major influence in the labor movement. The Carpenters and the Machinists, for example, ranked among the ten largest unions in 1897 (the Carpenters ranked second, the Machinists ninth) and are *still* among the top ten unions in terms of size (sixth and fourth, respectively). The building-trades unions, perhaps the heart of the craft union group in the AFL-CIO, together account for some 2.3 million members and are the third largest industrial group in the labor movement.

The CIO and Industrial Unionism

The craft-union model of labor organization, as embodied in the American Federation of Labor and its affiliated national unions, prevailed virtually unchallenged for half a century—from the founding of the AFL in 1886 to

[12] Data from Leo Wolman, *Ebb and Flow in Trade Unionism* (New York: National Bureau of Economic Research, Inc., 1936), p. 138.
[13] Estey, *op. cit.,* p. 353.

1935. But in 1935, the pre-eminence of the craft union as the type of organization best adapted to cope with the American economic and social environment was abruptly challenged by the establishment of a new organization which advocated a significantly different model of unionism.

The new organization was the CIO—the Committee for Industrial Organization—and its model was *industrial unionism,* whose distinguishing characteristic is membership based upon employment in an *industry,* regardless of occupation or skill, rather than upon employment in a particular skilled occupation, as in the craft union.

The cue for the launching of the CIO was appropriately dramatic—physical combat between two men who personified the differences between craft and industrial unionism.

At the 1935 convention of the AFL, during a discussion of industrial unionism in the rubber industry, "Big Bill" Hutcheson, president of the Carpenters Union and a staunch defender of the craft union position, raised a point of order to object that the industrial union issue had already been settled in favor of the craft unions.

John L. Lewis, president of the United Mine Workers and leader of the industrial-union forces within the AFL, snorted scornfully, "This thing of raising points of order all the time on minor delegates is rather small potatoes."

"I was raised on small potatoes, that's why I'm so small," shot back Hutcheson, one of the tallest and heaviest men in the convention.[14]

"Well, then, it's about time you were mashed," Lewis said, striking Hutcheson, and the two tangled and fell to the floor.

This clash marked the beginning of what proved to be a twenty-year division in the mainstream of the American labor movement. On November 9, 1935, Lewis, representing the Mine Workers, plus the presidents of seven other unions in the industrial union bloc, met and established the Committee for Industrial Organization, to encourage the organization of the unorganized workers in mass-production industries on an industrial basis.

Summoned before the AFL Executive Council for a hearing on charges of ignoring the decision of the convention and, worse, of committing the capital offense of dual unionism, Lewis and his cohorts in the CIO refused to attend. Told to disband the CIO or be suspended, they ignored the order. With that, the break was complete and the CIO, which later formalized its independence by changing its name to the Congress—instead of "Committee" —of Industrial Organizations, was on its own.

The contrast between the first years of the AFL and those of the CIO is as the contrast between night and day. In its first years, the AFL caused

[14] Report of the Proceedings of the Fifty-fifth Annual Convention of the American Federation of Labor, 1935, p. 727. Lewis' alleged reply to Hutcheson, as quoted here, is omitted from this Report.

hardly a ripple outside the labor movement; public attention was still riveted on the Knights of Labor. The activities of the newly formed CIO, on the other hand, not only attracted national attention, but were notable even in an era crammed with notable events.

The CIO's efforts to break into the mass-production industries were dramatic, to say the least. Indeed, as one writer put it, they comprised "the most remarkable episode in the annals of American labor."[15]

Within a single three-week period in early 1937, the CIO brought to terms the largest corporations in both the auto and the steel industries, and by thus penetrating to the very heart of the mass-production industries, paved the way for their subsequent, virtually complete organization. "The entire social structure of the country, its basic power relationships, were altered fundamentally . . . the United States had suddenly been propelled into the ranks of those nations in which the voice of organized labor counted."[16]

Symbolically, the CIO's first great success came in the auto industry, then, as now, the epitome of the mass-production industries. On February 11, 1937, after nearly six weeks of "the most critical labor conflict of the 1930's,"[17] General Motors, the largest of the big three automobile manufacturers, signed an agreement recognizing the United Auto Workers as the bargaining agent for its members.

And on March 2, while industry was still reeling from the shock of the General Motors agreement, the United States Steel Corporation, the bellwether of the steel industry, on its own initiative, and with no advance indications of its intention, signed an agreement with the Steel Workers Organizing Committee, through negotiations between Myron Taylor, chairman of the board of the corporation, and John L. Lewis.

As Walter Galenson, in his authoritative *The CIO Challenge to the AFL,* has written:

> . . . even the recognition of the United Automobile Workers Union by General Motors a week earlier did not have the impact of the steel settlement, since the GM agreement had been reached after a long and bitter sit-down strike, and with the most severe form of pressure exercised by the federal and state governments. Here, on the contrary, there had been virtually no government intervention and no industrial strife. The agreement was worked out by the parties themselves on a voluntary basis.[18]

The two cases present an interesting contrast. Originally chartered by the AFL in 1935, the United Auto Workers was dissatisfied at the restrictions

[15] Walter Galenson, "1937: The Turning Point for American Labor," Reprint No. 120 (Berkeley: Institute of Industrial Relations, University if California, 1959), p. 117.
[16] *Loc. cit.*
[17] Walter Galenson, *The CIO Challenge to the AFL, A History of the American Labor Movement, 1935–1941* (Cambridge: Harvard University Press, 1960), p. 134. This is the authoritative study of the rise of the CIO and its constituent unions.
[18] *Ibid.,* p. 93.

imposed by the AFL and switched its affiliation to the CIO in July 1936. Although aided and abetted by Lewis and the CIO, the Auto Workers was from the first an aggressively independent union, unwilling to take orders from anyone in or out of the labor movement. The weapon with which the UAW forced General Motors to capitulate was the controversial sit-down strike, a forerunner of the civil-rights techniques of the mid-1960's. Instead of the customary refusal to *come* to work, the sit-down strike was a refusal to *leave* work. In a sit-down strike, the workers occupied or seized a plant or factory and could be dislodged only by force. Subsequently declared illegal, and virtually abandoned even before the Supreme Court decision, the sit-down strikes of 1936 and 1937 were a key tactic in winning the General Motors strike—though intervention by both President Roosevelt and the Governor of Michigan was not insignificant.

The unprecedented success of the General Motors strike paved the way for the UAW to make rapid strides in the auto industry. Although UAW membership on the eve of the General Motors strike is not known, by June 1937, six months after the beginning of the strike, the union had won agreements with all the major producers except Ford (which was not unionized until 1941) and with many of the parts manufacturers, and claimed a dues-paying membership of 520,000.

And even though the sharp recession of 1937 brought the expansion abruptly to a halt, with unemployment cutting heavily into membership, the fact remains that, at the end of 1937, before it was even three years old, the UAW had catapulted into the position of fourth largest union in the United States.

In the summer of 1936, the CIO had established the Steel Workers Organizing Committee (SWOC), financed it with a $500,000 initial grant (according to one source, more money than had ever been pledged for a single organizing campaign), and provided its officers, Philip Murray and David J. McDonald, both of whom were later to become presidents of the Steelworkers Union. In short, the SWOC, unlike the UAW, was the creature of the CIO.

Following the peaceful capitulation of US Steel, the SWOC, too, made rapid progress and, by June 1937, claimed agreements with 142 steel companies and a membership of 376,000. But from here on, the path of the SWOC proved considerably more rocky than that of the UAW.

In May and June 1937, in efforts to expand its position in the steel industry, the SWOC struck the plants of the so-called "Little Steel" companies. In vivid contrast to the peaceful victory in US Steel, the Little Steel strikes were the scene of bitter and unsuccessful battles. In "the Memorial Day incident" alone, 10 people were killed and 125 others injured. And when the Little Steel strikes were closely followed by the recession of 1937, the expansion of unionism in the steel industry was effectively halted, not to be re-newed until the upheaval of World War II revived both the economic conditions in the steel industry and a climate favorable to unionism.

The CIO successes in both the auto and steel industries were by all odds its most impressive accomplishments. Quite aside from the speed with which they were carried out and the fact that they constituted penetration of what had been virtually unorganized industries, they demonstrated that industrial unionism would work where craft unionism had failed.

The CIO also penetrated other major industries in 1937—electrical and radio manufacturing, rubber, men's and women's clothing, textiles, meat packing, petroleum, and the maritime industry.

By the end of 1937, thirty-three national unions or organizing committees had affiliated with the CIO. Its total membership, according to recent esti-mates, was approximately 2 million, as compared to the venerable AFL's 3 million, and it could claim five of the ten largest unions.

At the time of the 1937 recession (one of the sharpest the country had ever experienced), the CIO was concentrating its efforts in the durable-goods industries. Although the recession had an especially severe impact on these industries, bringing CIO expansion grinding to a halt, the union's growth was resumed as business activity accelerated shortly before our entry into World War II.

In 1941, the organization of both the steel and auto industries was com-pleted—steel by virtue of an NLRB order to the recalcitrant Little Steel companies to comply with the Wagner Act, and the auto industry as a result of the decision of Henry Ford to deal with the UAW.

Wartime expansion, as usual, further stimulated the growth of unions, both CIO and AFL. CIO membership by 1944 was 3.9 million, more than double its strength in 1937. In 1953, during the Korean war, the CIO reached its all-time peak, with nearly 5 million members, of whom over a million each were in the auto and steel industries, and a quarter million each in the clothing, textile, communication, and electrical industries. When, in late 1937 and 1938, the CIO fumbled its drive for expansion, the AFL was galvanized into action and picked up the ball the CIO had dropped. In the course of its counterattack, the AFL recaptured its position as the dominant federation (if, in fact, it had ever lost it) by increasing its membership from 3 million in 1937 to 6.8 million in 1944. And while the CIO expansion had pretty much leveled off by 1947, the AFL continued to grow, from 8.5 mil-lion in 1947 to 10.5 million in 1955, at the time of the merger.

But the recovery of the AFL in no way indicated that the lessons of the CIO experience were ignored. Instead, many of the AFL's major unions abandoned the strict craft-union model and proceeded to adapt themselves to attract the semi-skilled worker, just as the CIO had. The rapid expansion of the Teamsters, Carpenters, and Machinists was due in large part to just such adaptation. Industrial unionism, whether under the aegis of the CIO or the AFL, had come to stay.

In weighing the factors which went into the emergence and success of the CIO, the leadership role of John L. Lewis, "perhaps the greatest entrepreneur of American Labor organizations," looms large. The stormy petrel of American unionism—who stepped down as president of the CIO only five years after he had founded it, who then took his union back to the AFL only to break with it again in 1947 and become independent of either federation, and who, in late 1941, less than six weeks before Pearl Harbor, could refuse a request from the President of the United States to send striking coal miners back to work while negotiations continued—was, as one writer put it, "as tough as the most anti-union employer; he possessed great administrative talents and had a flair for dramatizing himself and his cause . . . above all he was willing to play for high stakes. Lewis was very much in the tradition of the industrial tycoons who had built American industry, only he operated on the other side of the fence."[19]

Although the successful creation of industrial unions and the CIO can be attributed to Lewis' shrewd sense of timing and his vigorous and imaginative tactics in taking advantage of the stimulus of the Wagner Act, economic conditions, as well as the shift in public policy toward labor, made the circumstances ripe for a new form of labor organization.

Half a century earlier, when the AFL was founded, the United States was still in the process of transition from an agricultural to a manufacturing economy. Large economic enterprises had already appeared, to be sure (witness the Sherman Antitrust Act of 1890, designed to prevent excessive concentration of economic power), but much of what we know as the modern mass-production industries had not yet been developed.

In 1886, there was no automobile industry. The United States Steel Corporation was yet to be organized. The rubber industry was small. There were no radios. Plants were smaller, and no business employed workers in the numbers that are common today.

By 1935, on the other hand, the development of the mass-production industries such as automobiles, steel, rubber, and radios, had produced a situation which inadvertently gave to the unskilled and semi-skilled a source of economic power unknown when the skilled workers were first being organized by the AFL. That source of power, very simply, was the sheer power of numbers. While the skilled worker had long relied on the scarcity factor to make him difficult to replace and to give him bargaining power, the unskilled worker, individually or in small groups, was readily replaceable. But when we find 40,000 workers employed in a single establishment, as was the case

[19] Galenson, "1937: The Turning Point for American Labor," p. 112.

at the Ford Motor Company's Rouge plant in Detroit in 1935, then it makes little difference whether they are unskilled, semi-skilled or skilled—if they strike, their numbers alone make their prompt and effective replacement virtually impossible. In short, the sheer size of the modern mass-production enterprise provided the unskilled and semi-skilled worker with the power to back up their demands for improved wages, hours, and working conditions.

In 1937, the workers in the mass-production industries had the economic power, a newly favorable legal climate and strong leadership. Only one additional ingredient was needed—motivation. And they had it. In fact, "The principal ingredient which went into the success of the 1937 campaign was the strength of organizational sentiment among American workers," Galenson claims, adding: "Their belief in the efficiency of capitalism was all but destroyed by the shattering experience of the depression. It was not low wages which were fundamentally at the root of their dissatisfaction, for the CIO made its greatest headway in relatively high-wage industries. What workers rebelled against was the insecurity of their employment, the arbitrary character of management decisions affecting their lives, and the speeding up of work by companies seeking desperately to prevent operating losses."[20]

The Expulsion of Communist Unions[21]

Just as the AFL had been bothered at one time or another with the problem of corruption and racketeering in its affiliated unions, the CIO faced the problem of Communist influence in its affiliates. And both federations faced essentially the same problem in trying to cope with them—the fact that the autonomy of the national unions which belonged to them prevented direct intervention to solve the problem.

The origins of the problem of Communist influence in the CIO and its affiliates are complex, but two reasons for this problem deserve mention here. First, long before its successful adoption as the organizational model of the CIO, industrial unionism had been advocated as the proper solution for organizing the unskilled, principally by left-wing groups in the labor movement. While this in no way means that industrial unionists were all left-wingers or radicals, it was true that this long espousal by the left meant that when the industrial unions *were* established, the left-wing element tended to gravitate toward them, in preference to the AFL unions.

Second, it is generally believed that John L. Lewis, who was by no means naive about them, knowingly utilized the Communists in the great CIO organizing drives, confident that he could control them.

[20] *Ibid.*, p. 110.
[21] For the material on which this section is based, see Arthur J. Goldberg, *AFL-CIO, Labor United* (New York: McGraw-Hill, 1956), pp. 173–187.

But after the CIO's organization of the mass-production industries had reached its peak, and after the urgent demands of World War II had passed, it became clear that the Communists had become a powerful influence in unions whose membership represented perhaps one-third of total CIO membership. And, as the end of the war brought our alliance with Russia to an end, the divergence of interests between the Communist-dominated unions and the rest of the CIO became prominent.

As a result, the CIO in 1949 and 1950 expelled a total of eleven unions for following the program of the Communist Party in preference to the objectives of the CIO. The combined membership of these eleven unions was approximately 1 million members—nearly one-fifth of the total CIO strength at that time. Most of these members were subsequently recaptured by the CIO, in part by new unions chartered to replace those that had been expelled.

The expelled unions, on the other hand, fared poorly. By 1967, only two of the eleven (with a combined membership of 225,000) were still functioning as separate entities—the International Longshoremen's and Warehousemen's Union (ILWU) and the United Electrical, Radio and Machine Workers of America (UE).[22]

The impact of their expulsion from the CIO and the generally adverse effects of continued prosperity on the appeals of the Communist program appear to have brought Communist influence in the labor movement to a new low.

Changing Union Policy

The rise of the CIO and the industrial unions was not the only significant change in the structure and program of the labor movement to occur during the 1930's. The principle of exclusive jurisdiction, one of the pillars of AFL policy since the 1880's, was permanently modified. Two things account for its breakdown. Obviously enough, one was the creation of the CIO—with its establishment, the AFL no longer was the exclusive *source* of jurisdiction, and instead there were *two* major jurisdiction-granting federations, with no mechanism for preventing rivalry, competition, and overlapping jurisdictions.

Consequently, for nearly twenty years there were two auto workers unions —the UAW-AFL and its better known rival, the UAW-CIO. Today, there are three national unions whose primary interest is in the electrical industry —the IBEW, the IUE, and the UE. The list could be expanded substantially, but the point is clear; exclusive jurisdiction is a thing of the past.

The other major factor to affect the concept of exclusive jurisdiction was

---

[22] The American Communications Association merged with the Teamsters in October 1966, and the Mine, Mill and Smelter Workers affiliated with the Steelworkers in February 1967.

the Wagner Act of 1935. By giving the *workers* (through the secret-ballot election) the power to choose the union to which they would belong, the law in fact gave *them,* rather than the AFL or the CIO, the power to determine which union had jurisdiction over them. Under these circumstances, no union could be sure of exclusive jurisdiction.

The other pillar of AFL policy, the autonomy of the national unions, remained little changed. Although the CIO had created, staffed, and financed an international union—such as the Steelworkers—it generally recognized, as the AFL did, the basic fact that the national unions *were* autonomous organizations.

Labor's political posture also changed significantly during the 1930's, in part in response to the flow of social legislation and the increased role of the government itself, in part because of the political interests of the CIO, which as early as 1936, through Labor's Non-Partisan League, spent over a million dollars in the campaign to re-elect President Roosevelt, and in part because the great growth of union membership meant a corresponding growth in labor's political impact.

Perhaps the CIO's most lasting contribution to organized labor's increased political involvement came in 1943, with the establishment of the Political Action Committee—the PAC. Essentially, the PAC was designed to get at the grassroots, to inform the individual union member and to get him out to vote; it carried union political activity down to the precinct and the ward levels. Today, the techniques of the PAC are to be found in the AFL-CIO Committee on Political Education, or COPE.

Although organized labor cannot "deliver" the vote, since in the last analysis they have no sure means of controlling it, it is obvious that an organization with 15 million members (the AFL-CIO today) is going to carry more political weight than one of less than 3 million (the AFL in 1933). And, while the AFL-CIO today still maintains its technically non-partisan position—in February 1966, it announced that it would conduct a stepped-up campaign to "elect liberals to Congress regardless of party affiliation"—in practice, nonpartisanship has generally led to the support of Democratic rather than Republican candidates. The AFL-CIO is no political appendage of the Democratic party, but their relationship is a close one.

The AFL-CIO Merger

The big reunion between the AFL and the CIO took place on December 5, 1955, when, after a twenty-year separation, they merged into a single federation, the American Federation of Labor and Congress of Industrial Organizations. The new federation consisted of 138 national and international unions (108 from the AFL and 30 from the CIO), with a combined membership of 16.1 million (10.9 million from the AFL and 5.2 from the CIO).

Although efforts to heal the breach between the AFL and the CIO had begun almost immediately after the original split in 1935, certain specific factors appear to have contributed significantly to the actual consummation of the merger in 1955.

One contributing factor may be described as political—the passage of the Taft-Hartley Act in 1947. Both the AFL and the CIO were deeply disturbed by the Taft-Hartley Act; both roundly denounced it as a "slave-labor act" (because it provided for injunctions to force strikers back to work during "national emergency strikes"); and both vowed retaliation at the polls against its chief sponsor, Senator Taft of Ohio. When, to the chagrin of the two federations, the combined effect of their separate political campaigns against Senator Taft proved fruitless and he was re-elected, the question whether organized labor could continue to afford the luxury of rivalry at the price of political impotence became too persistent to overlook. The Taft-Hartley experience, in short, strongly suggested the practical necessity of combining forces if organized labor were to avert further legislative and political reverses.

Equally pressing, particularly from the CIO viewpoint, was the loss of membership it incurred as a result of its expulsion of the eleven national unions during 1949–1950 on charges of Communist domination. Collectively, these expulsions cost the CIO nearly 1 million members, or close to 20 per cent of its membership at that time. And quite aside from this loss, the fact was painfully apparent to the CIO that it had achieved only half the membership of the AFL. To be businesslike, it was evident that a merger of the two federations might effect substantial economies of scale, if only by eliminating duplication of effort and improving coordination.

Closely related to this was another problem of great concern to both the AFL and the CIO—the problem of "raiding," in which one union attempted to gain members, not by organizing the unorganized worker, but by attacking other unions and pirating their membership. Widely practiced by both AFL and CIO unions, the raids not only cost the labor movement millions of dollars that could better have been spent for expansion, but, as a joint AFL-CIO study revealed, had been largely futile as well.

Its analysis of National Labor Relations Board election results for the years 1951–1952 showed just how fruitless raiding actually was. As a result of more than 1,200 attempted raids, involving over 365,000 workers, only 62,000 workers changed unions. And since these changes were largely offsetting *exchanges,* the net result was that AFL unions gained the meager total of 8,000 members—less than 2 per cent of the number involved!

Accordingly, in December 1953, as a first concrete step towards merger, officers of both the AFL and the CIO signed a "no-raiding agreement" which was subsequently signed by sixty-five AFL and twenty-nine CIO national unions. As Arthur Goldberg, now Ambassador to the UN and former general counsel to the United Steelworkers has remarked, "The lesson to be drawn from that tabulation was so clear and the figures so overwhelming in their demonstration of the futility of raiding, that agreement at least in principle that it would be desirable to ban all raids between unions affiliated with the two federations was almost impossible to resist."[23]

Finally, and probably most important in the timing of the merger, was the change in the top leadership of both the AFL and the CIO. When the CIO split off from the AFL in 1935, the president of the AFL was William Green, and that of the CIO was John L. Lewis. In 1940, Lewis stepped down as president of the CIO (having promised to do so if President Roosevelt were re-elected) and was succeeded in that post by Philip Murray, his close associate in the United Mine Workers. Thus, both Green and Murray had been deeply involved in the tumultuous events surrounding the formation of the CIO, and while both may well have seen the need of recreating a single federation, neither could comfortably participate in such a move except on face-saving terms. As a result, so long as Green and Murray were at the helm they constituted a formidable barrier to the compromises and concessions necessary to bring a merger to reality.

In 1952 the situation changed. First Green and then Murray died—both less than a month after the election, on November 4, 1952, of the first Republican administration since Hoover's. Whether the prospect of a return to Republicanism was more than the two old Democrats could stand we cannot tell. Their successors, George Meany of the AFL and Walter Reuther of the CIO, while ardent supporters of their organizations, had played less critical roles in the original drama and could move forward toward the merger without a sense of personal surrender.

Even at that, the final negotiations for the merger took another three years, and it was not until December 1955, as we have noted, that the merger agreement was finally signed.

It is noteworthy that, at the time, the merger was the cause of widespread apprehension among the business community. The merger, it was reasoned, created a huge labor monopoly, half again as big as the AFL had been alone, and put it at the disposal of a single man, George Meany, the president of the merged organizations. And, thus, Meany, so it seemed to the alarmists, simply had to pick up a phone to call out, not 10 million workers, but 16 million who, at one fell swoop, would bring the nation's economy grinding to a halt and put it at the mercy of Meany and his cohorts.

This fearful prospect, of course, was groundless, for in the newly merged AFL-CIO, as in the former separate federations, each national and international union was to remain completely autonomous, with sole control over

[23] Goldberg, *op. cit.*, p. 77.

its actions. In fact, therefore, Meany had no more control over the Auto Workers the day *after* the merger than he did the day before, because even though the Auto Workers had become a part of the new federation, it still retained its autonomy and relinquished no authority to the new organization.

Nor did the fact that the two largest unions in the United States—the Teamsters and the Auto Workers—were now members of a single organization rather than of rival federations make any difference. Their economic value to each other remained unaffected (neither enhanced nor diminished) by the merger. Interunion cooperation has never depended much on formal affiliations or formal ties. Indeed, unions have helped each other economically and financially for many years, generally without regard for the small niceties of affiliation. Consequently, such changes in affiliation as were wrought by the merger had little effect on interunion relations.

The merger also had very little immediate effect on the ability and power of unions to make gains in collective-bargaining negotiations, because the bargaining power of individual unions depends on economic conditions in their particular industry or occupation and, in the last analysis, on their ability to conduct an effective strike, rather than on the size of the federation of which they are a part.

Events Since the Merger

The newly merged AFL-CIO shortly found itself faced with problems from an unexpected source—the Congressional investigations of corruption and misconduct in unions. The problems of corruption and racketeering in unions were by no means novel; they had plagued the labor movement at one time or another since 1900. What was unique about the problem in the mid-1950's was the extent of both public and official concern about it (particularly the latter).

To meet these problems, the AFL-CIO in 1956 and 1957 adopted a series of codes of ethical practices for union officials and backed them up with the power to suspend unions whose officers failed to adhere to them.

Expulsion of the Teamsters

By far the most dramatic application of these codes, of course, came in December 1957, with the suspension of the Teamsters Union for failure to oust Jimmy Hoffa. Today, ten years later, perhaps the most lasting lesson to be gained from the Teamsters expulsion is its emphatic demonstration that the historic doctrine of the autonomy of national unions is a fact, not a theory. For when the AFL-CIO leadership, embarrassed and annoyed by the McClellan committee's findings about Hoffa, wanted to get rid of him, they could only urge the Teamsters to remove him as President. The AFL-CIO was powerless to do so itself, for the Teamsters was (and is) an autonomous and independent decision-making body, and only the Teamsters Union had the authority to remove Hoffa.

When the Teamsters ignored its pleas, the AFL-CIO took the only step left to it—it threatened the Teamsters with expulsion unless Hoffa was removed. But this very act proved the AFL-CIO's lack of power to intervene; they could only impose the sanction of expulsion.

The result confirms this view. The Teamsters refused to oust Hoffa and were expelled from the AFL-CIO on a vote rather clearly split along craft and industrial union lines, with the industrial unions voting for expulsion, and the craft unions, particularly those in the building and construction trades—of which the Teamsters had been a long-time member—voting against it.

When the smoke had cleared, the AFL-CIO had lost 1.5 million members and some $750,000 in annual dues revenue and had failed in its objective of removing Hoffa. Their effort to dictate the Teamsters choice of officers had failed—they had been unable to overcome the real autonomy of the national union.

To add insult to injury, since the expulsion, despite all difficulties the Teamsters has continued to grow—and at a pace faster than the AFL-CIO.

After such a traumatic experience as this, it is little wonder that when the president of the Carpenters Union, the fifth largest union in the AFL-CIO, was accused of financial irregularities in connection with the Indiana highway program, the Federation had little heart to press for an ultimatum to the Carpenters similar to that issued to the Teamsters.

The First Decade

At this writing the AFL-CIO has come to the end of its first decade of merged existence. It seems appropriate, therefore, to review briefly what has happened during that ten-year period, in terms of both what the merger has done and what it has failed to do. Or, to put it another way, this is a good point at which to compare the actual consequences of the merger with the predicted consequences.

One of the most conspicuous failures of the merger has been its failure to expand its membership. In 1955, at the time of the merger, membership was 16.1 million. In 1964, according to the Bureau of Labor Statistics, AFL-CIO membership was down to 15.1 million. While the AFL-CIO has gained 500,000 members since losing the Teamsters, it is clear that net growth among the unions remaining in the Federation has been modest. Thus, with regard to the impact of the merger on the size of the labor movement, neither the hopes of the architects of the merger, nor the fears of the business community have been realized. According to one source,[24] when they merged, "the leaders hoped to double the total membership and increase labor's political influence"—a hope which has not come true.

And certainly the political record of the AFL-CIO since the merger does not fit the picture of a political behemoth, ruthlessly pushing aside all who stand in its way and relentlessly and irresistibly moving on to its objectives. Far from it; while it is true that after the merger the AFL-CIO achieved a significant political victory in engineering the defeat of right-to-work laws in several major industrial states in 1958, this triumph was short-lived, for in 1959, the Landrum-Griffin Act (sometimes known as the Labor Reform Act) was passed over the vociferous opposition of organized labor. And while it is true that labor campaigned vigorously for Johnson in 1964, and no doubt contributed to his landslide victory over Senator Goldwater, it is hard to consider labor's efforts as the key to Johnson's success. On balance, then, the political record of ten years of the AFL-CIO merger seems to be a standoff, at least in terms of *major* political objectives. And certainly, the inability of the AFL-CIO to push the Congress to repeal Section 14 (b)—the right-to-work provision—of the Taft-Hartley Act in 1964, 1965, and 1966 does little to justify the fears that were felt ten years ago.

In 1967, the AFL-CIO was facing a new threat to its stability and durability—the prospect of the United Auto Workers' withdrawal from it. Whether or not Reuther's resignation from the AFL-CIO Executive Council in February 1967 proves to have been the prelude to the secession of the UAW, it is evident that this was the most serious internal crisis since the Teamster case, if only because the UAW was the Federation's largest affiliated union.

[24] *The New York Times,* December 3, 1965.

3

Anatomy of the Labor Movement

The structure of the American labor movement—the interrelationships of its component parts—is as complex and intricate as its 18-million-member size suggests. Basically, however, this structure, or organizational anatomy, consists of three major segments or levels: the federation, the national or international unions, and the local unions. Each level has its own distinctive and special functions.

The Federation

At the center of the American labor movement (not at the head, because it does not control) is a single major federation, the American Federation of Labor and Congress of Industrial Organizations, generally referred to simply as the AFL-CIO. The AFL-CIO, like the United Nations, is a voluntary association, and is composed of free and autonomous labor unions. Accordingly, a union may be an integral part of the American labor movement without joining the AFL-CIO. While the AFL-CIO is therefore not all-embracing, it does include the great majority of national and international unions. In 1964, 128 of the 188 national and international unions belonged to the AFL-CIO. Their combined membership was 15,150,000, or nearly 85 per cent of total American union membership.[1]

A further analogy between the AFL-CIO and the United Nations may be noted. Just as individual citizens do not become members of the United Nations, individual workers do not become members of the AFL-CIO, but join one of the national or international unions affiliated with it. If their union should leave the AFL-CIO for any reason, as the Teamsters did in 1957, the individual workers' membership in their union is not changed, because they belong to the *union,* not the federation.

The AFL-CIO is, in short, a union of unions, not of individuals. Membership in the federation, in fact, is virtually confined to national or international unions. Although the federation does include a scattering of locals which belong to it directly, rather than to an international union, their membership is scanty—at last count only 56,000, or less than four-tenths of one per cent of total AFL-CIO membership—and their role is negligible.

Contrary to popular belief, the control of the 130 national unions affiliated with it is *not* centralized in the AFL-CIO, for it has long been a keystone of AFL (and now AFL-CIO) policy that in joining the federation a national union does not surrender its independence or sovereignty. In the terminology of the labor movement, the national unions are autonomous organizations, essentially free agents, setting their own policies, making their own decisions, and retaining full control over their own affairs. It is the officials of the national unions who decide whether to strike and what demands to make in negotiations, not the officers of the AFL-CIO. It has been well put, in fact, that the federation exists at the wish of the national and international unions, rather than the other way around. The federation has neither the formal authority nor the effective power to dictate the behavior of its constituent unions. The gnawing suspicion that George Meany, President of the AFL-CIO, could, if he wished, launch a strike of the 16 million members of the affiliated unions and bring the economy to a grinding halt by simply pushing the button is groundless.

The plain fact is that the AFL-CIO is not directly involved in the fundamental union function of collective bargaining. For all practical purposes that function is reserved for the national unions and, to a lesser extent, for the locals.

The primary role of the federation, instead, may be described as broadly political. The AFL-CIO is to organized labor roughly what the United States Chamber of Commerce is to business; it is engaged in lobbying, public relations, research, and education to present labor's views on countless prob-

---

[1] U.S. Department of Labor, Bureau of Labor Statistics, *Directory of National and International Labor Unions in the United States, 1965,* Bulletin No. 1493 (Washington, D.C.: U.S. Government Printing Office, 1966), pp. 45, 49. Unless otherwise noted, all statistical data in this chapter are drawn from this publication.

lems—not only on wages, hours, and working conditions, but also on topics ranging from public housing to foreign policy.

In addition, the federation performs various necessary functions within the labor movement. It charters new international unions, tries to minimize friction between affiliated unions and settle the disputes which occasionally break out between them, maintains a staff of organizers, and provides research and legal assistance primarily for unions too small to afford their own research staffs.

National and International Unions

After the federation come the 188 national and international unions which provide the basic framework of the American labor movement. National unions are more easily identified than defined; well-known examples of national unions are the Teamsters, the Auto Workers, the Steelworkers, the Carpenters, and the United Mine Workers. The Bureau of Labor Statistics, in compiling its biennial *Directory* of national and international unions in the United States, lists as *national* unions those having collective-bargaining agreements with different employers in more than one state and Federal employees unions holding exclusive bargaining rights; an *international* union is simply an American union which has members in Canada.

These 188 national and international unions range in size from the 1.5-million-member Teamsters Union, which is not only the largest union in the United States, but probably the largest single union in the free world as well, to the venerable International Association of Siderographers, AFL-CIO, which by 1964 had declined from its peak strength of 100 to a scant 31 members. (Siderographers are steel-plate transferrers, a printing trade.)

The great metamorphosis of the American labor movement in the past thirty years is reflected in the changes in size of the largest national unions. In 1933, just before the great expansion of union membership, the largest union (the United Mine Workers) had slightly less than 300,000 members, and only six reported 100,000 members or more. Thirty-one years later, the largest union had 1,506,769 members, two had over 1 million, six had passed the three-quarter million mark, and no less than 47 claimed membership of 100,000 or more.

With such disparities in the sizes of international unions, union membership tends to be concentrated in the largest unions, just as business assets or sales tend to be concentrated in the largest corporations. Thus, in 1964, the six largest unions together accounted for over six million members, or 33.5 per cent of total American union membership, and the ten largest unions accounted for 43 per cent of total membership. These levels of concentration in the six largest and ten largest unions are not new, however, and in fact are virtually the same as they were half a century ago.

Perhaps surprisingly, concentration in the *two* largest unions, at 14.9 per cent of total membership, is significantly lower than it was during the first quarter of this century, so much so in fact that the Teamsters, despite their 1.5 million members, now represent a smaller fraction of total union membership (8.3 per cent in 1964) than the United Mine Workers did during the forty-one years when *it* was the largest American union and accounted for an average of 11.2 per cent of total membership. In 1964, in fact, it would have required over 3 million members, or more than double the actual size of the Teamsters, to match the record share of 17.6 per cent of total membership held by the Mine Workers in 1901.[2]

While the evidence indicates unmistakably that the *concentration* of union membership is neither new nor increasing, the rise of individual unions to such great absolute size has undoubtedly been one of the prime factors in the development of the sentiment that union power needs to be checked and controlled; as is discussed below, however, size and power are not necessarily closely related.

If the federation performs a basically political function, the 188 national unions (whether members of the AFL-CIO or not) are the chief executives of the economic function—namely, collective bargaining. And since the American labor movement is distinctive for its emphasis on economic activities—a policy which goes back to Gompers—the national union, by virtue of its collective bargaining function, has emerged as the dominant force in the American labor movement.

To be sure, collective bargaining is not the sole prerogative of the national unions, for there are many cases in which local unions still play the decisive role in collective bargaining, chiefly in the building trades or service trades, where product markets are essentially local in character. But economic change and the broadening of product markets have tended to widen the area covered by a single collective-bargaining agreement (since, as we shall see, unions are forced toward applying uniform terms to all competitors) so that it often extends beyond the scope of the local union and shifts into the hands of the national union. As improved transportation and communications have hastened the growth of national markets at the expense of the local market, the national union has gained power accordingly.

Each national or international union has its exclusive jurisdiction, or territory, in which it claims the right to organize workers and control jobs. To use a business analogy, a union's jurisdiction is comparable to an exclusive sales territory or franchise. No union is to compete for the workers in the jurisdiction of another, although, as the frequency of jurisdictional disputes indicates, they often do.

[2] Marten S. Estey, "Trends in Concentration of Union Membership, 1897–1962," *Quarterly Journal of Economics,* Vol. LXXX (August 1966), pp. 347–349.

The jurisdiction of most national and international unions has been spelled out, at least initially, in the charter issued them by the AFL-CIO. (Of course, many charters long antedate the merger, having been issued by the AFL or the CIO.) But many unions have, on their own initiative, amended and modified the definition of their jurisdiction as the industries or occupations in which they operate have changed, or as their own objectives have widened.

Because in fact they represent something like a legal document, jurisdictional definitions are often extremely detailed, as for example that of the Teamsters Union, which claims jurisdiction over:

> all teamsters, chauffeurs, warehousemen and helpers; all who are employed on or around horses, harness, carriages, automobiles, trucks, trailers and all other vehicles hauling, carrying, or conveying freight, merchandise, or materials; automobile sales, service and maintenance employees, garage workers and service station employees, warehousemen of all kinds employed in warehouse work, stockmen, shipping room employees, and loaders, that is persons engaged in loading or unloading freight, merchandise, or other materials on to or from any type of vehicle; all classes of dairy employees, inside and outside, including salesmen; brewery and soft drink workers, workers employed in ice cream plants, and all other workers employed in the manufacture, processing, sale and distribution of food, milk, dairy and other products; all truck terminal employees; cannery workers; and other workers where the security of the bargaining positions of the above classifications requires the organization of such other workers.[3]

This broad jurisdiction has expanded from one basically limited as late as 1932 to local delivery drivers (of coal, ice, milk, and bread), until today the Teamsters is perhaps the closest American counterpart of the English *general* union, which in effect claims unlimited territory.

The aggressive imperialism of the Teamsters, in fact, has given rise to the joke (not entirely facetious) that "if it moves, it's a truck; if it has four walls, it's a warehouse."

And, indeed, the recent study, *Hoffa and the Teamsters,* makes it clear that from the outset of his activities in the union Hoffa's credo was to organize all the workers he could get his hands on and that in the 1930's and 1940's he often disregarded the traditional boundaries of Teamster jurisdiction; since then he has "explicitly rewritten the [Teamsters] International Constitution to eliminate such retarding limitations." [4]

In contrast to the practically limitless jurisdiction claimed by the Teamsters, that of the Marine Engineers Beneficial Association includes:

[3] *Handbook of Union Government Structure and Procedures; Studies in Personnel Policy,* No. 150 (New York: National Industrial Conference Board, Inc., 1955), p. 27.
[4] Ralph C. James and Estelle Dinerstein James, *Hoffa and the Teamsters: A Study of Union Power* (Princeton, N.J.: D. Van Nostrand, 1965), pp. 81–82.

All marine engineers who have been licensed by the Bureau of Marine Inspection, United States Coast Guard, to serve as such on vessels of the United States. Marine engineers regularly serving on commercial motor vessels operating in inland waters where license requirements have not been established by the Bureau of Marine Inspection in Navigation.[5]

The difference in the breadth and scope of these jurisdictional claims leads us to the fact that national and international unions can (in a broad sense, at least) be classified, according to the nature of their jurisdiction, as either craft or industrial unions. While these two categories, or structural types, can be expanded to six or seven,[6] the distinction between craft and industrial unions is a basic one.

Craft unions, of course, are those whose jurisdiction concerns a particular skilled *occupation* or occupations. Thus, among the traditional craft unions we would find the Carpenters, the Plumbers, the Bricklayers, and the Painters. Membership in such unions is a function of being employed in a particular occupation, irrespective of industry.

Industrial unions, on the other hand, define their jurisdictions in terms of particular industries or groups of industries, and membership is a function of employment in the industry, regardless of skill or occupation. The best-known examples of industrial unionism, no doubt, are the Auto Workers and the Steelworkers.

In practice, of course, there are many departures from, and exceptions to, these basic definitions. Industrial unions may not be all-inclusive of employees in an industry—for example, an industrial union may include only the production workers in an industry and make no attempt to organize its white-collar and office employees; or it may in fact be multi-industrial (as the Auto Workers union is). Craft unions may not, in fact, confine themselves to a single occupation, but go on to embrace a group of related occupations.

It would be pointless here to attempt a complete classification of union structural types; the essential point, as we shall see later, is that the question of structure has been a major source of controversy within the American labor movement; a union's structure directly affects its behavior, its policies and interests, and, in many cases, its long-run growth or decline.

Independent National and International Unions

Outside the AFL-CIO are what are generally referred to as the independent unions, which are the national and international unions not affiliated with the AFL-CIO.

[5] *Handbook of Union Government Structure and Procedures; Studies in Personnel Policy, op. cit.,* p. 23.
[6] Jack Barbash suggests that unions may be identified as "craft, multi-craft, trade, semi-industrial, industrial, multi-industrial, and nondescript." See Jack Barbash, *The Practice of Unionism* (New York: Harper & Row, 1956), p. 88.

The 60 independent national unions active in 1964 had a combined strength of 2,825,000 members, or 15 per cent of total American union membership. The reasons for their independence from the federation vary widely: Unions such as the Brotherhood of Locomotive Engineers and the Order of Railway Conductors and Brakemen never joined the AFL or the CIO and have always been independent, while the United Mine Workers withdrew from the AFL in 1947 in protest against the latter's policy on Taft-Hartley. A number of present independent unions were expelled from the CIO for alleged communist domination, and some were expelled from the AFL for alleged corruption or improper practices; the Teamsters Union was expelled from the AFL-CIO in 1957 in a fight over the presidency of Mr. Hoffa.

Local Unions

The third level in the union structure is the local union. Local unions, as a rule, are branches of national or international unions, although a few are affiliated directly with the AFL-CIO or are completely independent. All told, there are now approximately 74,000 local unions, ranging from the 40,000-member Local 600 of the United Auto Workers, which represents the workers at the Ford Rouge Plant in Detroit and is larger than many international unions, down to locals having seven or eight members, the minimum required by international-union constitutions to qualify for a local-union charter.

The bulk of local unions, like membership, is concentrated in a few national unions. Some 20,000 local unions, or more than 25 per cent of the total, are affiliated with the five national unions having 2,000 or more locals each. The 17 national unions having 1,000 or more locals each accounted for over 37,000 locals, or half the total number of local unions reported in 1964.

The vast majority (over 98 per cent) of local unions are subdivisions or chapters of one or another of the 188 national and international unions. But the relationships between a national union and its locals are much closer than between a national union and the Federation. Autonomy, such as that which the national union has *vis-a-vis* the federation, does not exist for the local union. Local unions are not only chartered by the national union, but may be disbanded, suspended, or put under administrative supervision (trusteeship) by the national union (subject to the terms of the Landrum-Griffin Act). Many union constitutions require local unions to obtain permission from the national union before calling a strike (or if not directly requiring it, make the payment of strike benefits contingent upon such clearance); representatives from the national union office may be sent to assist local unions in collective-bargaining negotiations or in handling grievances. In short, local unions generally lack the unrestricted decision-making authority of the national unions.

Like their parent national unions, local unions may be broadly classified as craft or industrial unions. The scope of local unions also varies according to the size and nature of the community in which they operate. Locals of an industrial union may be specialized according to occupation or industry (the Teamsters locals in major metropolitan areas tend to specialize according to industry) or by plant (as in the Auto Workers). In small towns, one craft local may cover the whole area.

Although it has yielded much of its collective-bargaining power to the national,[7] the local union has by no means been reduced to insignificance or impotence. For one thing, the local union is "where the boys are"—it reaches the worker "where he lives." The local union is the individual member's point of direct contact with his union; the performance of the local union is the basis on which he judges not only his local union, but, perhaps, his national union and the labor movement as a whole.

But if the local union doesn't bargain, what is there for it to be judged by? The answer is simple—the grievance procedure, the process by which the collective-bargaining agreement is administered and interpreted. It is the local-union officer, not the international representative or someone from the federation, who gets the individual member's complaints about how he is treated in the plant. And it is the local-union officer who, in effect, is responsible for winning or losing the grievance for the worker. If the grievance is settled in favor of the worker, the local—and through it the national union and unions generally—looks good to him; and if the grievance is lost, unionism suffers.

Similarly, active, interested, and effective local leadership tends to produce a favorable reaction from the members, and vice versa. In short, the local union *is* the union to the member. Its performance is the basis for his opinion of unions.

Independent Local Unions

Independent local unions are perhaps the most independent of all, for they are affiliated with neither the AFL-CIO, nor, like the majority of locals, a national union; their activities are generally confined to a single establishment, employer, or locality.

The 1,227 independent local unions responding to a Bureau of Labor Statistics survey in mid-1961 were estimated to have a combined membership of 452,000 in 1964.

---

[7] For a discussion of the role of local unions in the collective-bargaining process, see Leonard Sayles and George Strauss, *The Local Union* (New York: Harcourt, Brace and World, 1967), Ch. 2.

Interunion Relationships

State and Local Federations

The Federation has branches, or subordinate units, at both the state and local level. The former are known variously as state federations or councils (depending on whether the AFL or the CIO was the predominant force in that state before the merger) and the latter as city (or county) central labor unions. In June 1965, there were 50 state federations and 773 city federations (or local central bodies, as the AFL-CIO now calls them).[8]

The function of both state and city federations closely parallels that of the AFL-CIO itself: their primary concerns are state and municipal legislation, political action, and community relations—in short, lobbying and public relations.

Like the main federation, state and city central organizations are organizations of unions, not individuals. Local unions whose parent national unions are affiliated with the AFL-CIO are *eligible* for membership in their respective state or city federations (as are directly affiliated locals), but membership is neither automatic nor compulsory. As a result, only about 53 per cent of the nearly 62,000 locals in AFL-CIO unions were members of their state and local federations in 1964.[9]

A local union's decision to join or not to join the appropriate state or local body may be heavily influenced by intraunion politics. Thus, for many years, even before expulsion of the national union from the AFL-CIO rendered them ineligible, Teamster locals in the Detroit area tended to avoid membership in the Detroit and Wayne County Federation of Labor, apparently because it was controlled by a group unsympathetic to Hoffa. On the other hand, Hoffa was influential in the Michigan State Federation of Labor, and Teamster locals generally maintained membership in the state organization.

Trades Councils

In addition to coordinating lobbying and public relations efforts through the vehicle of the state, county, or city federations, unions frequently find it desirable or necessary to coordinate their economic activities as well, particularly in situations in which a number of unions face common economic problems. Perhaps the best known of these groups for coordinating activities between national unions or between their local unions are what are known as trades councils—literally, councils of unions active in a particular industry

[8] *Report of the Executive Council of the AFL-CIO,* Sixth Convention, San Francisco, California, December 9, 1965 (Washington, D.C.: American Federation of Labor and Congress of Industrial Organizations, 1965), p. 43.
[9] *Ibid.,* p. 54.

or group of related trades. Perhaps the archetype of all trades councils is that of the building and construction trades councils, which are found in 525 cities and 36 states and provinces (Canada).[10] In the Building Trades Council—which has its high-level counterpart in the Building and Construction Trades Department of the AFL-CIO—the locals of 18 national and international unions (including, for example, the Carpenters, the Electrical Workers, the Bricklayers, the Painters, and the Plumbers) deal with the mutual problems which they face because all are active in the same industry. These problems are not always labor-management problems; some of the thorniest, in fact, are jurisdictional problems between one union and another. But there is no doubt as to the effectiveness of their united action against the employer, as any contractor will agree who has had *all* union workers on his job walk off because of his dispute with members of *one* union.

The device of the Building Trades Council, in fact, provides the craft unions with one of the advantages of industrial unionism without sacrificing the values of the craft union. As such, it has proved a most valuable mechanism.

In addition to building trades councils (and similar councils in the metal trades, maritime trades, and the railroad industry) which are provided for in the AFL-CIO constitution, other less formal and less permanent relationships between unions may be developed for special purposes, such as coordinating negotiations with a common employer. A noteworthy example of this was the 1966 coalition of eight unions representing employees of the General Electric Company—an arrangement, incidentally, that was vigorously opposed by the company. Similarly, organizing campaigns may be conducted jointly by a number of unions, as in the Baltimore-Washington organizing campaign launched in 1963 by the AFL-CIO.

Intraunion Ties

Unions which are closer in structure to the industrial union than to the craft union but whose locals are specialized either according to the products handled or by occupations within an industry, require *intraunion* coordinating mechanisms. Thus, in many metropolitan areas there are what are known as *joint councils* or *joint boards*. Unlike the trades councils, which are composed of locals of different international unions, the joint councils consist of locals of a single national union, each with special problems distinct from the others, but all with the mutual bond of affiliation with the same union and the same basic industry. Typical are the Joint Boards of the International Ladies' Garment Workers and the Joint Councils of the Teamsters.

Thus, in New York, the New York Cloak Joint Board (which is active

10 *Ibid.*, p. 255.

in the coat and suit sector of the women's garment industry) includes some nine different ILGWU locals: Locals 117 (Cloak Operators), 10 (Cutters), 9 (Cloak Finishers), 35 (Cloak Pressers), 48 (Italian Cloakmakers), 23 (Skirtmakers), 82 (Examiners), 64 (Buttonhole Workers), and 102 (Cloak and Dress Drivers).[11] And 55 different locals, having a total of over 165,000 members, make up the New York City Teamsters Joint Council Number 16.[12]

Also, in the Teamsters, which is almost a "general" union, the advantages of sharing, on a national basis, common knowledge about special problems has been provided by the creation within this multi-industrial union of "trade divisions" and "trade conferences," such as the National Warehouse Division, the Bakery Conference, and the Brewery and Soft-Drink Division.

Similarly, many large unions are regionalized for administrative and executive purposes. But regionalization can serve more than administrative efficiency; the Western Conference of Teamsters, created in the early 1940's by Dave Beck (then simply the head of a Teamsters local union in Seattle), proved a political base for his election to the Presidency of the Teamsters in 1952, just as Hoffa's control of the Central States Conference of Teamsters has given him control of the largest bloc of votes in the International Union and made him politically almost invulnerable.

[11] *Report of the General Executive Board to the 31st Convention,* Atlantic City, New Jersey, May 23, 1962 (New York: International Ladies' Garment Workers' Union, 1962), p. 23.
[12] *The International Teamster,* January 1966, p. 9.

4

The Management of Unions

It is customary to describe the internal organizational structure of a labor union in political terms and to compare it with the organizational structure of a business firm, paying particular attention to the ultimate sources of authority in each case.

The Power Structure

Accordingly, the organizational structure of the labor union is referred to as democratic, because its chief officers are *elected* either by the general membership of the union or by their delegates at national union conventions, rather than appointed by their predecessors or their fellow officials. Top union officers are therefore responsible and accountable to the membership and, in the last analysis, must satisfy them if they are to stay in office. The final authority therefore rests in the hands of the members, not the officers. In this case, power flows from the bottom of the organizational pyramid to the top.

In the business firm, on the other hand, final power and authority rests either with the owners or stockholders or with *appointed* officials to whom it has been delegated; power flows from the top down, and its organizational structure is described as *authoritarian.*

It should be emphasized that these labels are intended to be neither critical nor complimentary, but simply descriptive of particular relationships between the upper and lower levels of a hierarchy. The fact that the labels may seem complimentary or critical reflects the tendency of Western societies to place a higher value on democratic than on authoritarian government or administration.

Structure alone, of course, is not the only determinant of an organization's political and administrative style. Union officials, no less than other politicians, are adept at building political machines and utilizing a democratic structure to their advantage. Thus, the reader may recall flagrant examples of dictatorial union leadership (as well as impressive illustrations of democratically run businesses), for it is quite true that the character of an organization can be significantly affected by the way in which it is administered. But that does not alter the basic point of the analysis, which is that the *organizational structure* of one institution is democratic while that of the other is authoritarian.

The elections through which the membership exercise their ultimate control of the union are generally held at local union meetings or at the national union convention. In a relatively few cases, voting for union officers is done by referendum or by mail ballot. The national union convention is often both a legislative and a judicial body, providing for a vote of the membership on dues and assessments, on constitutional changes, and, in some cases, on appeals from executive decisions made since the previous convention, as well as for election of officers.

But the election is a periodic event which, according to law (the Landrum-Griffin Act), national unions must hold at least every four years. In the interval between elections, therefore, the administration of the national union is generally left in the hands of an executive council or executive board, similar to the board of directors of a corporation. And between executive-board meetings, the actual operations of the union are carried out by the president and his executive officers, with the assistance of various and sundry staffs, boards, and committees.

Quite aside from his constitutional powers, the general president of a national or international union is likely to wield great *de facto* powers. This stems from the fact that, as some writers have put it, the president is, in effect, the commander-in-chief of an army[1]—a fighting organization whose predetermined single objective is to advance the economic interests of its members. In many cases, the president is the chief union negotiator in bar-

---

[1] A. J. Muste, "Army and Town Meeting," in Bakke, Kerr, and Anrod, *Unions, Management, and the Public,* 3rd ed. (New York: Harcourt, Brace and World, 1967), p. 168.

gaining with management. In this capacity he controls the key function of the union, guiding it through its most crucial moments. He must make the command decisions; he must determine what action is necessary to meet the requirements of the situation. Union policy, set by convention or by other means, can provide him with guidelines, and union members can hold him accountable for his actions and approve or reject them, but he is the chief executive and, like any other executive, he must make decisions when they are called for.

Furthermore, because he has the facts and figures at his disposal and has personally had the opportunity to judge and interpret management's behavior at the bargaining table, the union president has the advantage in answering the critics and doubters among the members and is generally able to convince the membership of the wisdom of his actions.

Ultimate Authority of the Membership

The ultimate authority of the rank and file is no mere textbook proposition, however, but an operational reality, as has been vividly demonstrated in recent years.

In a majority of unions, collective-bargaining agreements negotiated by union officers and staff must be ratified by the membership before they become effective. Of course, ratification is often just a *pro forma* ritual, because, as we have suggested above, union leaders politically astute enough to be elected to office are likely to be able to persuade the membership to accept their recommendations. But the formality must still be observed, and since the passage of the Landrum-Griffin Act, with its emphasis on union democracy, there has been an increasing tendency for the membership to reject proposed collective-bargaining settlements as unsatisfactory and to send their leaders back to the bargaining table—for more.

Thus, the Philadelphia regional office of the Federal Mediation and Conciliation Service, in June 1966, reported a 22 per cent increase in its case load over the previous year and attributed a significant portion of the gain to union members' refusal to accept contract terms won and recommended by their officers.[2] While the Mediation Service saw them as related to prosperous economic conditions, the rejections point up the significant extent to which the membership *does* exercise final authority over the union's stand in collective bargaining.

And perhaps no year in recent union history gave more dramatic evidence than did 1965 of the fact that the rank and file is still able to exercise its power to determine who its officers shall be, and even established leadership may be voted out of office. In that year, we witnessed the defeat of the

[2] *The Philadelphia Bulletin,* June 19, 1966.

incumbent presidents of the United Steelworkers of America, the third largest union in the country, and of the International Union of Electrical, Radio and Machine Workers, as well as those of several smaller national unions.

It would be unrealistic to regard these as simple manifestations of popular discontent, when instead they may be more appropriately described as palace revolutions—the outcome of power struggles at the top. But the fact remains that these changes have been carried out by the mechanism of a vote of the membership, and the factions fighting for control have had to conduct their contest in the open and wage their fight in the form of a fight for voter support—a true political contest.

Membership Participation and Apathy

But this evidence that the membership can and does play a vital role in union government should not be interpreted to mean that the well-known problem of membership apathy—the tendency of the rank-and-file member to let George do it and leave the decisions to his leaders—has been solved.

Whatever the reasons for this apathy—whether the issues are becoming so complex that they cannot be properly evaluated by the ordinary member; whether traditional union emphasis on economic objectives leaves the membership with the attitude that the union is simply providing an insurance function or a public-service function, which it is up to the administration to perform as best they can; whether the sheer size of the typical union today leaves the member feeling that his vote cannot change things anyhow; or whether the union meeting simply cannot compete for the member's spare time with the many recreational activities available to him—whatever the reasons, it is an observed fact that attendance at union meetings is usually confined to a small fraction of total membership. Only 10 or 15 per cent of the members may turn out for an ordinary union meeting, and even such critical decisions as election of officers or the ratification of a proposed collective-bargaining settlement may bring out a bare majority of members.

The agreement between the Transport Workers Union and the New York City Transit Authority, reached in January 1966 after a twelve-day subway and bus strike that brought threats of new legislation from President Johnson, was subsequently ratified when the membership, in a mail ballot, voted 15,683 to 2,170 in favor of acceptance. Although the vote was therefore more than seven to one in favor of agreement, the total vote cast represented only 55 per cent of the 33,000 members involved.[3]

When it comes to turning out to vote in the election of union officers, still another factor must be borne in mind if we are to understand member be-

[3] *The New York Times,* February 8, 1966.

havior. The election process in American unions differs from the typical election for public office because the candidates, especially at the national union level, generally run unopposed. Unions typically do not have a two-party political system, with an incumbent party and a recognized and accepted opposition party. Only one national union, the Typographical Union, has a two-party political system.

Lacking a system which "legitimizes" opposition, incumbent officials are generally nominated to succeed themselves, and they generally face the final stage of election unopposed. Nomination, accordingly, is often equivalent to election. Offered no choice, and unlikely to benefit from rejection of the candidate at the last minute, the members' apathy and indifference to the outcome of the election under such circumstances seems inevitable. Even in the 1965 election of the president of the Steelworkers Union, which offered the voters the rare opportunity of a contest between two experienced union officers, only about 60 per cent of the members eligible to vote actually did so. On the other hand, when the choice is whether or not they are to *belong* to a union, workers are far from apathetic. Thus, in NLRB representation elections, conducted in the eight years 1958–1965, approximately 90 per cent of those eligible to vote have done so.[4] Indeed, it is consistent with the economic orientation of business unions that the response of the membership to decisions involving their union appears to be a function of the economic impact of the issue.

Thus, when strike authorization is sought from the membership, it is generally approved by a substantial margin. This consistent tendency to support the leadership on the strike issue is understandable, however, when it is realized that to reject a strike call is not simply a vote of no confidence in the leadership; more seriously, it amounts to a decision on the part of the members not to fight, a decision to send their leaders to the bargaining table not only unarmed, but conspicuously so, for management is publicly informed of this fact by the outcome of the vote. Thus, because it is contrary to the worker's self-interest to weaken his union's bargaining position, a vote to reject a strike is rare.

But to reject a contract settlement is quite a different matter. The member is likely to see this as simply a way of *improving* his position—for the effect of rejection is to send his leaders back for more. The risks seem negligible to him and the possibilities of improving his position appear good.

Similarly, the well-known resistance of members to dues-increase proposals—perhaps the most difficult proposals to push through a union convention—arises from the adverse effect these increases, at least in the short-run, have on their pocketbooks.

[4] National Labor Relations Board, *Annual Report, 1964*, p. 19; and *Annual Report, 1965*, p. 19.

To put membership apathy into historical perspective, it should be noted that this problem is neither recent nor a function of the growth of large unions, as one might suspect. Instead, we find the Webbs reporting complaints of union apathy in London as early as 1890:

> Only in the crisis of some great dispute do we find the branch meetings crowded, or the votes at all commensurate with the total number of members. At other times, the Trade Union appears to the bulk of its members either as a political organization whose dictates they are ready to obey at Parliamentary and other elections, or as a mere benefit club in the management of which they do not desire to take part.[5]

And to put the alleged apathy of union members into a current context, the fact is that the union member takes about as much part in his union—when major decisions are involved—as the average citizen does in national political decisions. Thus, in the 1964 presidential campaign, only 70 million of 114 million eligible voters (or 62 per cent) actually exercised their right to cast a vote—roughly the same as the proportion that voted in the Steelworkers election in 1965.

The point we wish to stress, in any case, is that high levels of participation, as measured by voting activity, are typical of the individual *neither* as union member *nor* as citizen. The individual union member is as active in exercising his right to vote in his union as he is in national political affairs, or in other organizations to which he belongs. And while we may feel that his union is of more immediate concern to the union member, and that he *should* take more part in it, it is *his* union, not ours; he must decide how he wants it run.

The Union Managers

The men who run the union from day to day and set the course of action it is to take (subject to the veto of the membership), are its officers and staff, who may properly be considered as the union managers. Indeed, lest we appear to be stretching a point to talk of managers in a union context, it should be noted that in at least one union, the International Ladies' Garment Workers, the chief executives of local unions are known as *managers*.

Understandably, the most distinctive (though by no means the most important) qualification for elected union officers is essentially political rather than managerial—they must have worked their way up from the ranks and spent some time in the trade or industry whose workers they represent.

Unlike corporate executives, whose managerial talents are readily transferable and who can move with relative ease from one industry to another,

[5] Sidney and Beatrice Webb, *The History of Trade Unionism,* rev. ed. (New York: Longmans, Green and Co., 1920), p. 465.

union leaders rarely, if ever, shift from one union to another, less because their managerial talents are too specialized than because rank-and-file attitudes still discourage it. The complete professionalization of union management has not yet taken place.

Salaries

The compensation of union officers has been a matter of considerable public interest, much of it frankly critical of the levels to which it has risen. And now that the Teamsters have raised President Hoffa's annual salary from $75,000 to $100,000 there may be another wave of criticism—or envy.

Hoffa's salary, however, is the highest paid any American union officer, just as it was when he was paid $75,000 annually. The salary of the typical union officer is much more modest. In 1958, when the top union salary was $50,000 annually, a BLS study of 75 international unions revealed that the most common salary for the top officer of a national union was between $10,000 and $15,000 a year.[6]

In trying to appraise union officers' salaries, it quickly becomes apparent that there is no objective standard upon which they can be judged and no figure which can be reasonably established as to what union officers *ought* to be paid for their services. Should they be paid according to the size of their union? If so, Hoffa *should* receive the highest salary in the labor movement. But even if we accept that criterion, we are still faced with the question: What should the highest salary in the labor movement be? How can we justify Hoffa's salary of $100,000 as head of the Teamsters Union? Why, for that matter, shouldn't he get more? We *might* look at the cost per member of Hoffa's salary. With 1.5 million members, the cost *per member* of Hoffa's salary is 6⅔ cents per year—hardly a heavy burden and, perhaps, even a low price for vicarious adventure. No matter which way we appraise the problem, there is no answer.

In one way, of course, unions have only themselves to blame for the criticism of their officers' salaries. For years, a standard item in the union organizer's bag of tricks was to make critical comparisons between the pay of the business executive and that of the production workers in his plant.

The author remembers hearing a United Auto Workers official commenting on the salaries of General Motors executives and rapidly calculating for a rapt membership that the president of GM made more in one year than they could expect to earn in a lifetime—with the obvious implication that no one was worth *that much* more than the man on the assembly line. The differential between Hoffa's salary and that of the average teamster is less

---

[6] U.S. Department of Labor, Bureau of Labor Statistics, *Union Constitution Provisions: Election and Tenure of National and International Union Officers, 1958*, Bulletin No. 1239 (Washington, D.C.: U.S. Government Printing Office, 1958), p. 21.

dramatic—perhaps on the order of ten to one, rather than say forty to one— but the same criticisms the unions have used with such relish to whip up sentiment for organization have now been turned against them.

Tenure

Closely related to the interest in union officials' salaries is the question of how long they do, and should, serve in office. Here again, it is the exceptional cases which attract attention. It is well known, for example, that the Teamsters Union was led by one man for 45 years. Dan Tobin became president of that union in 1907,[7] when it had only 36,000 members, and continued in office until 1952, when it had over one million members. John L. Lewis assumed the presidency of the United Mine Workers in 1919 and remained for thirty-nine years, until 1958.

As in the case of officer's salaries, there is no standard as to the proper length of service for union officials, any more than there is for corporate officers, many of whom hold their positions for comparable periods of time.

But because of the union's democratic structure and the union emphasis on its contribution to democracy in the workplace, the question can be raised, with somewhat more force and validity than in the corporate case, whether long tenure on the part of union officers is compatible with the democratic image the union claims for itself.

The evaluation of this problem involves both constitutional technicalities and economic factors. The constitutional technicality arises from the way in which union constitutions are worded. An analysis of 111 national union constitutions, applicable to 96 per cent of all union members in 1957, found that although the maximum term for union presidents was 5 years, "no constitution limited the number of terms a president could serve."[8]

Union constitutions, accordingly, impose no effective barriers to long tenure. And beyond a certain point, length of service in a leadership position tends to become self-perpetuating, whether in a union, business organization, or political position. The cult of personality becomes increasingly evident, and, as time goes on, criticism of union policy tends to be regarded as criticism of the individual leaders and comes perilously close to disloyalty, as well as organizationally risky for the critic.[9]

The problem was brought into focus at the 1965 convention of the AFL-CIO, which found itself faced with the threefold problem of an aging top leadership, no effective mechanism for bringing up replacements, and no

---

[7] *The International Teamster* (July 1966), p. 5.
[8] U.S. Department of Labor, Bureau of Statistics, *op. cit.,* p. 20.
[9] For a penetrating analysis of this question, see John D. Pomfret, "Labor and Its Leaders," *The New York Times,* April 8, 1965.

orderly way to effect the transition of power from one generation of leaders to another.

Thus, in 1965, the Executive Council of the AFL-CIO (between conventions the highest governing body in the Federation), consisted of twenty-seven members, nine of whom had been heads of national unions when they assumed a seat on the Council, but who had since reached retirement age or had been defeated in an election.[10]

Subsequently, eight of these nine council members (the exception being Harry C. Bates, the then 83-year-old former president of the Bricklayers Union and a historic figure in AFL circles), whose average age in 1965 was 67, were unseated and replaced with eight active union presidents whose average age was 58.[11]

The problem of replacing top union officials is compounded by several factors—officers' reluctance to exchange their income, prestige, and power for virtual oblivion (a sentiment they share with leaders of many other organizations); the lack of any effective system for training replacements; and the fact that the internal organization of the union is more likely to discourage and to punish leadership ambitions among the younger men than to encourage or reward them.

But there is another side to the problem of the length of service of top union officials. The business union, as we have seen, gives its top priority to effective performance—to delivering the goods and to reaching its members through their pocketbooks. Efficiency, not democracy, in its internal affairs, is therefore the guiding factor in union government. And although it is inseparable from the self-interest of the officials concerned, a strong case can be made that, given the emphasis on efficient and effective union leadership, long service (up to a point, at least) of union officers works to the advantage of the members.

The essential point is simply that experience in office pays off in greater bargaining skill, a better grasp of the economics of the industry, and better understanding and judgment of the management opponents. If there were a direct and continuous correlation between length of service and bargaining competence, it would of course be an almost unanswerable argument for long tenure. Certainly, there is persuasive evidence that the Mine Workers benefited materially from the long service of John L. Lewis or that the rank-and-file Teamster, for that matter, may well benefit economically from Hoffa's re-election. At the national-union level, particularly, it seems likely that frequent turnover of top officials would generally be more detrimental than beneficial for the membership, although it would be more democratic. It takes time for even an experienced union officer to learn to make the

10 *The New York Times,* December 2, 1965.
11 *Ibid.,* December 14, 1965.

most efficient and effective use of his new responsibilities. When David Mc-
Donald became president of the Steelworkers in 1952 on the death of Philip
Murray, he found himself immediately faced with final responsibility for
negotiating a new contract with the steel industry. And although McDonald
had been in top executive circles of the union since its founding in 1937, the
terms achieved in his first negotiation as president were widely reported as
not wholly pleasing to the membership, whose reaction was to charge this
performance up to inexperience, but to say, in effect, "it had better be good
next time."

Despite the apparently unvarying tendency toward long service in office of
international union presidents, we are presently in a period of unusually high
turnover in the leadership of major unions as a result of both hotly contested
elections and, in addition, the fact that many well-known labor leaders are
retiring, either by choice or as a result of a slow but increasing trend on the
part of unions to adopt compulsory retirement standards.

Thus, in the eighteen months ending June 30, 1966, the nation witnessed
a turnover in the presidency of four of the ten largest unions—the defeat at
the polls of the presidents of the Steelworkers and the International Union of
Electrical Workers, the passing of compulsory retirement age of A. J. Hayes,
president of the Machinists, and the retirement of David Dubinsky, president
of the International Ladies' Garment Workers' Union.

The Decision-making Process in Unions

Political and sociological factors, as well as economic ones, have a great
deal to do with *how* unions make collective-bargaining decisions and with
what those decisions are.

Because union officials are elected rather than appointed, they must, regardless of the effectiveness of the political machines they may develop and
regardless of the extent of formal membership participation in union decision-making, maintain the support of the rank and file, who can (and do,
if they are dissatisfied) reject hard-won contract settlements or, as a last
resort, vote their officials out of office or turn to other unions.

Maintaining rank-and-file support in an economically oriented institution
such as the American business union is largely a matter of delivering "More,
now," for this is what the worker wants—and this is the standard by which
he judges the performance of his union leader.

But the crucial question for the union leader is: How *much* more is
enough? This question, in fact, lies at the heart of union decision-making in
collective bargaining, for the generalization that unions seek "more" gives
us only the direction in which unions are driving. How does the union leader
or the union negotiator decide that one offer is acceptable and another—

sometimes only cents an hour lower—is not? What are the criteria by which the union negotiator determines that it is politically safe for him and other union officers to make an agreement with management?

Comparisons

One answer to this question is to be found in comparisons. The rank-and-file union member obviously cannot make a complex economic analysis of the "package" his union leaders deliver at contract time. But he can and does compare what his union gets for him with what other unions get for their members. And since the union member, like anyone else, has a great desire to keep up with the Joneses, a satisfactory settlement, for him, is one which is as good as or better than the other fellow's—while one that is not is unsatisfactory. *This* is the standard by which he judges the performance of his union leaders; this is the criterion he applies to their record.

For example, the steelworker may compare himself to the autoworker. If Walter Reuther wins a ten-cent-an-hour increase for the Auto Workers, this becomes the critical point for the Steelworkers officers, who feel constrained to win ten cents an hour, or more. A nine-cent increase would be unacceptable, for it would be "not as good" as the Auto Workers settlement. More to the point, for the Steelworkers officers to settle for less than the Auto Workers would imply (whether justified or not) that *they* were "not as good" as Reuther; it would be politically unsafe, if not necessarily disastrous. An increase of *more* than ten cents, on the other hand, would be grounds for rejoicing—a political victory of real value.

Although comparisons may be most compelling when they involve industries closely related economically to the member's own, comparisons may be made regardless of economic differences between industries. Economic conditions in the steel industry may be substantially different from those in the auto industry, but the workers in the two industries, nevertheless, are likely to expect comparable increases (it should be emphasized that we are talking about comparable *increases*—not identical terms of employment in both industries.)

It is obvious, of course, that the Steelworkers do not have to compare the collective-bargaining achievements of their union leaders with those of the Auto Workers. They could compare them with the Mine Workers, or the Teamsters, or the Carpenters—in fact with the performance of any of the 180 or more international unions currently operating in the United States.

Here is where union leadership comes into play. Part of the union leaders' role is to influence the comparisons his members make. Indeed, the selection of suitable and advantageous comparisons is not only the way he convinces his membership he has done a good job, but it is an important aspect of collective bargaining, for the latter is essentially a matter of negotiating over *which* comparisons are right—the union making comparisons which justify its demands and the management negotiators pressing those which favor their position.

In any case, the union leader's success in convincing the members of the validity of comparisons he offers them may be instrumental in determining whether the agreement he has won is acceptable to them. Of course, once a particular set of comparisons is "sold" to the membership by the leaders, it tends to become the standard comparison. The union leader, therefore, tends to operate within a fairly fixed set of comparisons. Because he has "sold" them to his members himself in previous years, he knows in advance just what comparisons the members are likely to make.

The Steelworkers compare with the Auto Workers, in the last analysis, because at some time past, the Steelworkers officers made this comparison. But once having made it, the leaders are stuck with it. They know that the comparison will be made, so the Auto Workers settlement becomes the minimum that the Steelworkers must get. Rather than accept less, they will strike.

Economic Factors

Economic factors *do* enter into the picture, of course, sometimes through the comparisons we have been discussing. Thus, if economic conditions in the steel industry at negotiation time are notably better than in the auto industry, it will affect the workers' comparison—they will expect their "package" to be not just as good as, but better than the Auto Workers' package.

One of the factors in the determined stand of the Machinists Union during the six-week-long airline strike in the summer of 1966 was the fact that the exceptionally favorable profit position of the airlines made an above-average settlement a political necessity for the union, whose top leadership was new (having taken office in 1965) and, from the point of view of the membership, untested.

Response to Membership Pressure

The airline strike also points up the very real dilemma of the union leader involved in a strike in a crucial industry. The public is bound to be highly critical of the inconvenience, hardship, and economic loss resulting from the strike and is likely to assume that the problem is basically a matter of stubbornness and indifference to the public welfare on the part of the union leader. What the public generally fails to realize is the extent to which the union leader's obduracy in such situations is the result of pressure from his membership—the result of their insistence that he hold out for more. Seldom has this point been more forcefully demonstrated than during the airline strike, when a tentative settlement, negotiated under White House auspices

and announced by President Johnson himself, was rejected by the membership by a margin of more than two to one.[12]

And while there is a constant expectation on the part of the public that
in this situation a union leader will yield on his demands and be "responsible" to the public interest, this expectation completely ignores the fact that
the union leader's first responsibility is to his members. This is not merely a
matter of loyalty, it is a matter of the most direct self-interest, for it is the
members, not the public, who will decide whether the union leader keeps
his job.

Ironically enough, the sensitivity of union leaders to rank-and-file pressures has probably been increased by the Landrum-Griffin Act—more, perhaps, by its general focus on the rights of the members, than in any specific
provision—whose passage may in part be attributed to vigorous pressure
from employer groups.[13] But having seen the effects of greater union democracy (not the least of which may be higher costs to them), employers are
showing signs of wishing for a return to one-man rule in unions—to "responsible" union leaders with final authority to make a binding decision
which management can be confident will not be rejected by the membership.
Thus, for both management and the public, it is evident that union democracy in the form of membership power to veto collective-bargaining decisions
is not an unmixed blessing.

The role of comparison in union decision-making sheds light on another
point that is widely misunderstood. Unions do not really push in each negotiation for "all they can get." Dramatic though it sounds, the fact is that
unions want to leave something for next time. Even more to the point, the
union leader generally is interested in getting only enough to satisfy his membership; to fight for more than that is simply a waste of his time and energy.

Of course there are occasions and situations in which the union leader
wants to outdo other leaders by as wide a margin as possible. But generally,
the union leader wants to live to fight another day; he wants to have something to get next year and the year after. Politically, if he meets the standard
of comparison or exceeds it somewhat, he is safe.

If it takes hard bargaining to win a ten-cent package, it is harder to win a
twelve-cent or fifteen-cent package. If, in the judgment of the union negotiators, ten cents is politically safe, they are not likely to push for twelve
or fifteen cents—because, in economic terms, they are as interested as the
next man in achieving their goals (in this case membership approval) at the
lowest possible cost. The union leader may misjudge the membership sentiment, as we have seen, but membership rejection of proposed contracts is
illustrative of a corollary of the point we have just made. It is the rank and

[12] *Ibid.*, August 1, 1966.
[13] A. H. Raskin, "Rumbles from the Rank and File," *The Reporter* (January 28, 1965),
p. 28.

file, contrary to popular opinion, that are often the most aggressive and demanding, rather than the leadership. It is more often a case of the rank and file being the militants and the leadership trying to restrain them, than of the leaders dragging unwilling members out on strike against their wishes or insisting on holding out for gains unsought by the members.

And there is a reason for this. Leaders not only tend to grow away from the rank and file as time goes on (and the problem is doubtless aggravated in the larger unions), but also they become, through repeated dealings with management, inevitably more aware of the complexities of the problems over which they are bargaining and more aware of the substance of management's position. No sell-out to management is required for the union leaders to become, as time goes on, more conservative than their members in the interpretation of what can be obtained.

Bargaining Within the Union

The decisions confronting union officers concern not only how much to demand from management, but also how much is enough to satisfy the membership. Equally important is what the package is to consist of—how the gains won from management are to be distributed. A ten-cent package can take a number of forms and vary in a number of ways: in terms of its division between direct wage increases and fringe benefits; in terms of how the direct wage increase is distributed as between, say, skilled and unskilled workers; and so on, almost *ad infinitum*.

The distribution of these gains is no minor matter; it is of crucial importance to the internal politics of the union. The union is not only an agent for the negotiation and settlement of the conflicting interests of management and labor, but it is equally a mechanism for resolving and balancing the conflicting interests among its members.

George Taylor expressed it concisely when he said that one of the main functions of a union is "to discern, reconcile, and then represent the diverse and often conflicting demands and interests of its membership."[14]

One such problem of reconciling conflicting needs within its own membership is that confronting the United Auto Workers. As is typical of an industrial union, the great bulk of the UAW's membership falls into the semi-skilled category. Political necessity therefore dictates that the collective-bargaining program of the union and the distribution of collective-bargaining gains reflect this fact. At the same time, however, there is a small but impor-

---

[14] George W. Taylor, "The Role of Unions in a Democratic Society," in *Government Regulation of Internal Union Affairs Affecting the Rights of Members*. Selected Readings prepared for the Subcommittee on Labor and Public Welfare, United States Senate, by the Legislative Reference Service, Library of Congress (Washington, D.C.: U.S. Government Printing Office, 1958), p. 19.

tant group of highly skilled workers—diemakers, model makers, etc.—whose economic leverage as a group cannot be overlooked. So the union periodically has to negotiate special or supplementary benefits for the skilled workers to compensate for the fact that the regular negotiations tend to be tailored to fit the needs of the semi-skilled majority. Thus, in July 1966, the union asked General Motors, Ford, and Chrysler (though not American Motors) to consider granting wage increases to its 250,000 skilled-trades members, despite the fact that the union contract was not to expire until September 1967. This was done because the skilled workers were unhappy at the large gains being made by the construction workers (a group to whom *they* compare themselves) and saw their position, *relative* to semi-skilled production workers, deteriorating.[15]

One of the advantages of the craft-union type of organization, in terms of decision-making, is that, because of the essential similarity of the problems that members face, the community of interests of their members is relatively great and conflicts of interest relatively small. In the industrial union, on the other hand, the variety of jobs held by the membership inevitably produces a variety of interests among them, many of them unavoidably conflicting. The leadership of the craft union, accordingly, is probably called upon to devote less of its time to resolving *internal* differences of interest among its members than is the leadership of the industrial union; craft union administration appears to be less complex than that of the industrial union.

The experience of the United Auto Workers affords another example of the problems of balancing different needs within a union. The General Motors strike of 1964, which closed assembly plants for over two months immediately after the 1965 models had been introduced in September, is generally conceded to have occurred, not because either the leaders or the membership were dissatisfied with the general economic gains offered by the company, but because the rank and file felt that in the course of several successive contract negotiations "local issues" had been subordinated to national ones. While the problem undoubtedly represented the focus of a number of factors, it is nonetheless believed that Reuther felt impelled to permit a strike to resolve such local problems as washroom time and smoking privileges because they had become too important to the members to set aside any longer.

And a strong case can be made for the view that in spite of his undeniably effective over-all collective-bargaining record as president of the Steelworkers Union, David McDonald's loss to I. W. Abel by a narrow margin was due to the way those gains were distributed. The evidence indicates that McDonald actually led Abel by a slight margin among Steelworkers in the United States and that the 10,000-vote margin by which Abel won was just about the size of the *Canadian* membership of the union, which allegedly

[15] *The New York Times,* July 16, 1966.

voted against McDonald because they felt that during his thirteen years in office he had consistently discriminated against them in the distribution of collective-bargaining gains. Whether their belief was justified is less important than the fact that the experience demonstrates how crucial *internal* bargaining can be.

Centralization of Decision-making: The Shift of Power to the National Unions

Another important aspect of union decision-making is the long-run trend toward centralization of power and authority in the national unions, primarily in the form of increased control of collective-bargaining decision-making and execution. This centralization of union decision-making is due not to any single factor, but to the combined effect of a number of factors.

One of the key factors responsible for this continuing shift of power from the local to the national union is an economic one—the growth of a national market for products. Because this is so fundamental to an understanding of how unions operate, let us look at the problem in detail.

In competitive industries, the presence of nonunion firms is a barrier to further gains for union members and a threat to the security and survival of the union. Accordingly, out of sheer economic necessity, unions tend to expand toward their economic limit—the organization of all firms competing in a particular market, whether it is a product market or a service market. And having organized them, the union must then push to eliminate wage differentials among them in order to take wages out of competition.

Given these economic pressures to expand to the limits of the competitive market, it is obvious that anything which affects the extent of that market, anything which affects the area of competition, will affect the extent of union activities.

What has happened and is continuing to happen is that the extent of the market is changing—the area of competition is becoming broader and broader. As our transportation system and our communications have improved, product markets have spread, so that today the majority of products compete and are sold in regional or national markets rather than local markets, as was formerly the case.

The broadening of the product markets, however, means more than just a further expansion of union organizing objectives or a further expansion of the number of firms subject to a single collective agreement. Sooner or later, the expansion of the product market extends the area of competition beyond the jurisdiction of the single local union. It brings firms in one locality into competition with firms in other localities. And when this happens, the economic terms of the collective agreements made by local unions in one community become immediately relevant to locals active in the same industry but in other localities.

To put it another way, when the product market has extended beyond the boundaries of the single community, bringing two or more communities into a single competitive area, the union is faced with a repetition of its original problem—it still needs to "take wages out of competition." But now the problem changes; it is no longer simply a matter of wage differentials between union and nonunion firms. When several different locals of the same national union are making collective-bargaining agreements on wages and all are operating within a single competitive area, the existence of differentials between one *union* wage level and another creates the same problem as the wage differential between union and nonunion firms—low union rates are a drag on the further advancement of higher ones. The solution to the problem of differential wage settlements made by locals within a single competitive area is coordination—insuring that all locals within the area of competition apply uniform terms so that there are no differentials and none of the problems that the differentials create.

While there are many ways in which local-union bargaining can be coordinated (in fact, some of the structures noted in Chapter 2 owe their existence to the need for such coordination), perhaps the most common solution is simply for the national union to take control of the negotiation process. This is what has happened: the extension of the product markets has created a situation in which coordination of collective-bargaining patterns of different local unions is required, and this has led, increasingly, to the assumption of control over collective bargaining by the national unions.

In those industries in which the product market has remained predominantly a local one, the local union tends to remain in control of collective bargaining, more or less independent of the national union. But in industries whose product market is national in scope, the responsibility for collective bargaining over economic issues (although, because of the veto power of the membership and the pressures involved in internal bargaining, not always *control* of it) has tended to shift to the national union, leaving the local union with primary responsibility for bargaining over local issues and for day-to-day administration of the contract.[16]

It is intriguing to speculate whether the combination of trends toward greater democracy within unions and a revival of interest in noneconomic issues (which may be relatively neglected in national bargaining) might also have modified the distribution of power within the labor movement, shifting it away from the national and toward the local union.

The building trades and the auto industry provide practical illustration of the differences between industries in which the local union still controls collective bargaining and those in which control is held by the national union.

Decision-making in the building trades is decentralized not because of some stubborn determination by local building trades union officials to resist

[16] For an authoritative discussion of the role of the local union, see Leonard Sayles and George Strauss, *The Local Union* (New York: Harcourt, Brace and World, 1967).

the loss of control to the national union, but because the product market of the building trades remains (and seems likely to remain) predominantly local in character. The buyer of housing is not likely to pull up stakes and move lock, stock, and barrel to buy a house in another city simply because housing is cheaper there. The fact is, he wants housing in his present community. And because the consumers are essentially unable to respond to *price* differentials between cities, the union, in turn, has no need to fear an adverse impact from *wage* differentials between cities. Builders in one city are not in competition (for these purposes) with those in another. And since the national union is not concerned with wage differentials between locals in different cities, there is no pressing economic need to coordinate their collective-bargaining decisions, and the local unions have retained control of the collective-bargaining process, making literally hundreds of separate collective-bargaining decisions, each limited to a particular local market. Indeed, it is this very decentralization that makes the building trades (for example) the despair of Administration attempts to enforce its wage guidelines as well as an obstacle to the elimination of racial discrimination in employment (see below, p. 69).

The auto industry, on the other hand, operates in a national product market. This, of course, is because automobiles, unlike houses, are shipped from the point of assembly to the retail market. And while assembly plants are located in many cities, the fact that the product is shipped long distances to its final market means that the competitive impact of wage differentials would reach and carry adverse effects as far as automobiles can be economically shipped.

Were each local to negotiate independently and without reference to what other locals are doing, it would clearly pay the manufacturer to concentrate production in those plants where labor costs were lowest, so they could produce a given car at the lowest cost. But this would be detrimental to the employment and wage prospects of workers in the high-wage plants. In this case, then, the national union is compelled by economic factors to provide coordination between the decisions of different locals—in the form of national control and negotiation of master agreements applicable to all locals, regardless of where they are. And this is why the government's guidelines could, if it wished, be applied with some degree of effectiveness in the auto industry—because in the auto industry collective-bargaining decisions are highly centralized, so that the government's pressure could be concentrated at a single point.

The increasing shift of collective bargaining on economic issues from the local union to the national union is also stimulated by factors other than the pressure to prevent the corrosive effects of wage competition between locals.

Political or sociological factors may be equally important, for, regardless of the economics involved, workers think it only fair that an employer follow the policy of equal pay for equal work. So when a single employer has plants in different cities, the workers in each doing similar work, the pressure for *internal* consistency affects not only the employer but the union as well. If a number of local unions are involved, the necessity for coordinating their negotiations with a *single* employer becomes another factor pushing control toward the national union.

In the automobile industry, for example, the Auto Workers do not negotiate with General Motors, Ford, Chrysler, and American Motors simultaneously, but one at a time. But in 1961, the General Motors negotiation alone affected 310,000 workers in 131 plants located in 66 cities in 18 states.[17]

Obviously, consistent treatment of members at General Motors requires a high degree of coordination between the many local unions involved (among other devices for accomplishing this is the National General Motors Council, which consists of representatives of UAW locals at these 131 plants); it has been achieved by national-union intervention and control of bargaining with the corporation.

Where a company's decision-making is centralized and basic policy decisions (such as collective-bargaining decisions) are not delegated to plant managers, the local union is confronted with management representatives who have no authority to decide on their demands and who have to pass these demands on to "headquarters" for a decision. Accordingly, local union officers turn to *their* headquarters—the national union—so that those with the same degree of authority on both sides of the table can do the actual negotiations.

Still another factor pushing power and control into the hands of the national union is that of the growing complexity of collective-bargaining problems. This has led unions, like their business counterparts, to make increasing use of staff specialists—economists, lawyers, accountants, etc.—to prepare the materials for collective bargaining. The sheer expense of maintaining such staffs is beyond the resources of most local unions; the expense of negotiating with big business is so great that only national unions can afford it.

This complex of factors—economic, sociological, administrative—then, has tended in the past to push an ever-increasing share of the collective-bargaining process into the hands of the national union. And since collective bargaining is the central activity of the American business unions, it is customary to say that the national union is the backbone of the American labor movement—the basic member of the structure.

Today, however, the rapid growth of the service industries, whose markets are predominantly local and whose business organizations are more often

[17] Robert M. MacDonald, *Collective Bargaining in the Automobile Industry* (New Haven: Yale University Press, 1963), p. 6.

medium to small in size, suggests that the trend to centralization of the collective-bargaining function in the national unions may be ending and that, as union growth is increasingly concentrated in the service industries, local unions may play an increasingly important role in the bargaining process.

Meeting Institutional Needs

In the course of the extensive scrutiny to which unions and their internal activities have been subjected since the end of World War II, it has often been alleged that the union is not exclusively devoted to protecting and promoting the welfare of its members, but that some of its energies and resources are spent on its own behalf, as an institution to further the goals of the organization, as distinct from those of its members.

There is no question that this is a valid comment. The point is, however, that the union, like any other institution, is interested in its own survival and development. And indeed it must be, for it can hardly serve the interests of the members, either well or poorly, if it goes out of existence. So institutional survival and the pursuit of institutional goals are not in themselves inimical to the interests of the membership; in fact, they are essential for the welfare of the members.

Like so many of those involving union administration and internal government, the questions here are whether the share of union resources devoted to the welfare of the organization rather than that of the members is *excessive,* and whether, in any case, the methods or procedures used by the union in its self-interest are "good" or "bad."

Admission policy

Compulsory membership   One such institutional goal of unions is the so-called union security issue, or the question of compulsory union membership. Strictly speaking, what is involved are efforts by unions to make union membership a condition of employment—compulsory for those who want the job in a unionized plant. While anyone who is opposed to it can avoid the requirement by simply not working in a shop or plant where union membership is a condition of employment, union membership can be *virtually* compulsory, either because the worker cannot find equally good work elsewhere or, even more compelling, because there are no openings elsewhere. This point is very relevant, as we shall see later.

The union security issue is hardly new, for it was a part of the Philadelphia Cordwainers case in 1806. Most recently, however, it has been the basis of the fight over the right-to-work laws and the repeal of Section 14(b) of the Taft-Hartley Act, which is the legal footing of these laws. It should be made clear at the outset that the term "right-to-work" has nothing to do with a guarantee of employment, as it seems to imply, but is simply a euphemism for the direct prohibition of compulsory union membership.

In the last analysis, of course, the numerous arguments concerning compulsory union membership may be viewed simply as rationales of the real issue, which is simply the power struggle between labor and management. In this view, managements fight against compulsory unionism because they are opposed to union growth and increased power, which they see as a threat, no longer to their survival—or to the American way of life—but to their freedom to manage as they see fit. Unions fight for it, not only because it greatly simplifies their organizing efforts, but because they believe, as management does, that it is an avenue to their growth and power.

The argument and the debate may not be entirely wasted, however, for it is designed among other things to influence public opinion and to tilt legislation in favor of one view or the other. There are two basic arguments in the fight over compulsory unionism; one the union's argument, the other, management's. The basic union justification of compulsory unionism is the "free rider" argument, which stems from the fact that the Wagner Act and the Taft-Hartley Act make the union which wins a representation election in a plant the representative of *all* the workers in the bargaining unit, members and nonmembers alike. (Furthermore, these laws prohibit employers from discrimination in the terms of employment between union members and nonunion workers.) Consequently, in plants where the union bargains with the employer but lacks a compulsory membership requirement, nonunion employees *must* get the same wages and fringe benefits that union members do, to comply with the law. The nonunion workers thus get the benefits of unionism without paying its costs (fees and dues); they are "free-riders."

Under these circumstances, of course, the union argues that since the law requires that *all* workers in the bargaining unit get its benefits, it is only fair that *all* should share in the costs—by being required to belong to the union. The union slogan might well be a switch on that of the Boston Tea Party: "No representation without taxation."

The chief management argument against compulsory unionism (and it is a *management* argument more than a nonunion *worker* argument) is that it interferes with the worker's freedom to choose whether or not he wants to belong to a union; that it is undemocratic and dangerous for a private organization such as a union to be allowed to force a man to join against his wishes in order to hold a job. Certainly this seems plausible enough; it is an argument designed to appeal to the true liberal, the defender of individualism. But there is a flaw in this argument, for the truth is that an essential ingredient of the effective functioning of the modern business organization is *standardization*—and not the least of the factors to be standardized are the terms of employment.

It is not an arbitrary management but the industrial process itself which dictates that employees start to work at specified times and that their work schedules be uniform. The point is, then, that generally speaking, the individual employee has no choice as to the terms of employment in a particular plant. He cannot pick and choose the days he works, the hours he works, or the wages he will get; if he did, the result would be chaos. He takes what is offered, or leaves it. And if only one firm has openings for his particular talent, he is likely to take what they have, even if *some* of the terms of employment are unsatisfactory to him. Economic necessity can make the terms of employment compulsory, whether the firm is unionized or not. And making union membership one of the terms of employment simply adds another requirement to those already imposed by the facts of industrial life. It *is* an additional restriction on the workers' freedom of choice, no doubt about it. But removing *that* restriction will not restore the worker's freedom of choice. It will not leave the worker free to choose his terms of employment; it simply means *one less* restriction on his freedom.

Indeed, it may be argued, without being too sophisticated, that if the worker is a member of a union, he at least has a voice in the demands it makes on the employer and at least *some* voice in determining the terms the employer establishes for him. While the increase in the freedom of choice he gets in this manner cannot be quantitatively weighed against the freedom he loses by being required to join the union, it does seem that they tend to offset each other.

But there is a point at which the freedom issue is valid. There is a *conflict* of freedoms involved—the conflict between the freedom of the union members to work in a shop without nonunion workers and the freedom of the nonunion worker to remain nonunion.

Where there is such a conflict of freedoms, an accepted way to settle the issue, since there is no objective way to settle it on its merits, is to submit it to a vote and allow the principle of majority rule provide the answer. This was done in the case of the union shop elections between 1947 and 1951, when a majority of workers involved voted in favor of the union shop.[18]

More recently, the issue of compulsory unionism was put to a vote on a broader scale when right-to-work laws were submitted to the voters in a number of states. In terms of practical politics, the outcome of these votes has been perhaps less a matter of the persuasiveness of arguments than of the composition of the population. In states with a large industrial and urban population, a large proportion of workers are union members who vote against right-to-work proposals because they regard them as attempts to weaken organizations which they find beneficial. And generally speaking, their votes have proved decisive.

[18] See p. 80.

This point was convincingly demonstrated in 1958, when, in six states—California, Colorado, Idaho, Kansas, Ohio, and Washington—right-to-work proposals were on the ballot. In the predominantly industrial states of California, Ohio, and Washington, as well as in Colorado, the proposals were defeated. Only in two agricultural states, Kansas and Idaho, did a majority vote for them.

The result is that the nineteen right-to-work states are the predominately agricultural and rural states, in which the industrial worker is a minority and unions are relatively weak.

Restrictions on membership   Having been criticized for years for infringing upon the worker's freedom *not to join* a union if he chooses (by their insistence upon making union membership a condition of employment), unions are, perhaps ironically, also being criticized, especially in the last decade, for their tendency to restrict admission to membership, thereby infringing upon the worker's freedom *to join* a union if he chooses. Specifically, attention has recently been focused on the fact that many unions have pursued either formal or *de facto* policies of discrimination against Negroes.

Restrictive membership policies, in fact, have a long history in the American labor movement. The skilled-crafts unions in particular have taken pains to restrict entry to their trades in order to limit competition for jobs and to maintain or raise the price of their members' services.

Viewed *solely* in these terms, restrictive admission policies are simply another facet of business unionism, one which reflects a shrewd grasp of the advantages businessmen have found in creating barriers to entry in their industries.

But viewed in the context of our prevailing concern for civil rights, such behavior, at least if it involves racial discrimination, is no longer acceptable —it violates both public policy (the Civil Rights Act of 1964) and public spirit. In *this* conflict of freedoms, the freedom of the individual to admission to a union on a nondiscriminatory basis takes priority over the freedom of union members to choose their colleagues.

A variety of devices are used to limit and restrict membership. The simplest and most extreme is the closed union, which refuses to admit anyone. Closed unions may still be found in the building trades, as in the case of the Philadelphia building trades local which, when picketed in 1964 by members of NAACP on the grounds that it discriminated against Negroes by refusing them admission, protested, with a certain logic, that they had not been engaged in discrimination because: "We don't take in *any* new members, regardless of color."

Unions which ordinarily follow less restrictive policies may temporarily close their books to new members when existing members are unemployed.

Closely akin to closed unions are those which admit only relatives of members. The Stagehands Union in New York City, for example, was recently ordered by the State Supreme Court to admit three men who charged that, although they had been working on a permit-card basis, they had been denied full membership because of union nepotism.[19]

Another device for limiting entry to the trade has been apprentice regulations, which are intended, among other things, to insure proper training of craftsmen. But the apprentice program may become a device for discriminatory admission practices, for a man who is not admitted to apprenticeship is not likely to become a union member.

None of these policies is *specifically* discriminatory, as between one group of applicants and another. But unions have discriminated, and do specifically discriminate, against women, Communists, Fascists, and subversives, and, most importantly, against Negroes.

Racially discriminatory admission policies have included constitutional barriers by national unions, such as those of the Brotherhood of Locomotive Engineers, which (until its 1966 convention voted to eliminate them in compliance with a court order) provided that no one could become a member "unless he is a white man" and required that applicants be sponsored by three members—a ritual allegedly used to bar nonwhite applicants.[20] The chartering of separate segregated local unions for Negroes and other non-whites has also been common, especially in the South.

Such constitutional and administrative barriers in national unions are now rare; indeed, the Locomotive Engineers' may have been the last formal racial barrier in any national union constitution. But the problem of discrimination at the local level has been harder to eliminate. In particular, authoritative opinion suggests that efforts to end racial discrimination in the building-trades unions will remain difficult because of local autonomy in the building trades, nepotism as a basis for acquiring union membership, the economic power of the building-trades unions, and the traditional belief in the need to preserve limited job opportunities for a limited membership.[21]

Industrial unions, in contrast to craft unions, have generally found their interests more effectively served by an inclusive rather than a restrictive membership policy. Since, in the union shop, which is the common union security provision among industrial unions, the employer hires whom he pleases, the union goal is for *all* new employees to become members, for it is control of numbers rather than of a hard-to-replace skill that gives the industrial union its bargaining power.

Furthermore, it would be self-defeating for industrial unions to pursue a discriminatory admissions policy, for, as Slichter, Healy, and Livernash point out: ". . . in industries where a large number of Negroes, Puerto Ricans, Mexicans, or Orientals are employed, the industrial unions must take an

---

[19] *The New York Times,* July 20, 1966.
[20] *Ibid.,* July 15, 1966.
[21] Ray Marshall, "Equal Employment Opportunities: Problems and Prospects," *Proceedings* (IRRA Spring Meeting, 1965), p. 467.

agressive stand against discrimination or give up the prospect of organizing the non-whites."[22] As a consequence, the industrial unions have long been leaders in the drive to eliminate discrimination in employment and in union membership.

With the passage of the Civil Rights Act of 1964, of course, unions are prohibited from excluding individuals from membership because of race, color, religion, sex, or national origin; from segregating their membership on such bases; and from discriminatory practices in connection with apprenticeship programs. The public policy is clear; it only remains to be enforced.

Fees and Dues

If what unions *pay* their officers is at one end of the financial spectrum, what unions *cost* their members is at the other.

The money costs of union membership are of two types. First and most important are those which affect all members, i.e., initiation fees and periodic dues (including occasional special assessments for one purpose or another). Second are those designed to meet special situations or problems and which affect only a small minority of members—transfer fees and work permits.

Union dues typically run between $3 and $4 a month, or less than $50 a year. The most recent and comprehensive figures available—the data collected in 1960 from the financial reports of more than 48,000 local unions filed to meet the requirements of the Landrum-Griffin Act—show that over half of the local unions charged dues of less than $4 a month, the most frequently reported figure being between $3 and $4. Barely one per cent of local unions reported dues higher than $10 a month, and only 9 of the 48,000 local unions reported dues over $25 monthly.[23]

Tying this information to the fact that in the industries employing the great bulk of union members—manufacturing, construction, coal, railroads, and telephones—average hourly earnings in 1960 ranged from $2.26 to $3.14, it may be seen that the typical monthly dues payment cost the union member, in real terms, about two hours work.

Generally speaking, the level of dues (and of initiation fees as well) is related to the earnings in the occupation. Skilled-craft unions tend to have higher fees than industrial unions composed chiefly of semi-skilled workers. And high dues may also include premiums for special purposes such as death benefits and retirement, disability, and unemployment benefits.[24]

[22] Sumner H. Slichter, James J. Healy, and E. Robert Livernash, *The Impact of Collective Bargaining on Management* (Washington, D.C.: The Brookings Institution, 1960), p. 53.
[23] *Report of the Bureau of Labor-Management Reports, 1960*, pp. 26–27. The rest of the data on union costs in this chapter are from this source.
[24] Philip Taft, *The Structure and Government of Labor Unions* (Cambridge: Harvard University Press, 1954), p. 68.

Although union dues may seem modest enough when judged by such standards, proposals to raise dues are likely to encounter opposition from the members. Indeed, the recent hotly contested election in the Steelworkers Union was preceded, in 1956, by a contest between President McDonald and a previously unknown local union officer, Donald Rarick, who based his campaign almost entirely on opposition to a dues increase which had been adopted at the previous union convention.

Initiation fees run somewhat higher than dues, in part because they are a one-shot charge, rather than a recurring one, and in part because they may be used to limit membership in a union and thus assist it in maintaining control of a particular labor market. On the other hand, it is not unusual for unions to waive initiation fees as inducement to join, especially for low-income groups.

Financial reports indicate that in 1960, although 28 local unions reported initiation fees as high as $500 or more, the majority charged $10 or less, and the most common initiation fee was $5.

Transfer fees may be regarded as a special form of initiation fee, since they are charged for transferring membership from one local union to another. In 1960, less than 20 per cent of reporting unions imposed transfer fees, and, of those that did, the most frequent figure was $1 or less.

Work permits, which are essentially dues and/or initiation fees for temporary members, are not a common practice, being used by less than 15 per cent of reporting unions. Like regular membership dues, the most frequently reported work permit fee in 1960 was between $3 and $4 a month.

5

The Behavior of Unions

The mainstream of the American labor movement consists of what are generally referred to as *business unions*. Traditionally, the term business union has been used to distinguish unions whose goals are primarily economic from those whose objectives are primarily political or ideological. Business unions are chiefly concerned with what they call "bread and butter" issues—with winning better economic conditions for their members in the form of higher wages and fringe benefits, shorter hours, and better working conditions—rather than with what they have derisively called the "pie in the sky" objectives (long-run, "ultimate" goals) of the Socialists and Communists.

The purpose and objective of business unions may be summed up in the two words, "More, now." As Samuel Gompers, first president of the American Federation of Labor, testified before a Congressional committee in 1914, "the best possible conditions obtainable for the workers is the aim," and when these conditions are obtained, "why, then, we want better . . . today and tomorrow and tomorrow—and tomorrow's tomorrow."[1] That description is as accurate today as it was half a century ago.

[1] See Leon Litwack, *The American Labor Movement* (Englewood Cliffs, N.J.: Prentice-Hall, 1962), pp. 40–41.

Market Orientation of Unions

But perhaps more to the point is that today's business unions are primarily market-oriented; they concentrate on improving the terms under which their members *sell* their services. While it is true that they are concerned with a wide variety of problems and issues which affect the worker away from the job (from education to housing to foreign policy), they focus the bulk of their resources and energies on one major target, the improvement of the conditions of their members at work.

Collective Bargaining

Unions accomplish this objective, in general, by negotiating directly with the businessmen who *buy* their members' services, rather than by placing primary reliance on government intervention and legislation. This process of negotiation between a union and the management of a business firm over the terms of employment is known as collective bargaining. And so far as business unions are concerned, unions and collective bargaining are two sides of the same coin—inseparable.

Collective bargaining is thus a way of setting the price of labor in the market. But it is more than that. Collective bargaining is *the process by which unions share in making business decisions;* not all business decisions, to be sure, but those decisions involving the terms of employment and the price of labor. It would be a mistake to assume that unions are simply advisory bodies who suggest to businessmen what their members would like and let it go at that. On the contrary, once management has recognized the union as the representative of its employees, it has, perhaps unwittingly, but nonetheless effectively, yielded its right to make unilateral decisions with regard to the terms of employment and conditions of work in favor of sharing them with the union. By means of collective bargaining the unions become one of the institutions through which business is conducted. *This* is the real significance of business unionism.

The impact of collective bargaining is not exclusively economic, however. It is also a major contribution to democracy in industry, for it provides the industrial worker with a mechanism for participating in making the rules under which he works.

Collective bargaining introduces democratic processes into the administration of business organizations in a number of ways. It establishes a system of checks and balances against the arbitrary exercise of management authority. It brings with it not only a new way of *making* rules, as we have shown, but also a new way of day-to-day *interpretation* of the rules, known as the grievance procedure. The grievance procedure, which may properly be considered as a continuation of the collective-bargaining process, is essentially a judicial process, an appeals machinery to insure that the law of the plant, as represented by the collective-bargaining agreement, is properly applied and interpreted. The decisions reached through the grievance procedure become part of the common law of the plant, as it were.

And when the grievance procedure terminates in provision for voluntary arbitration, as is the case in nearly 90 per cent of all labor-management agreements today, union and management of their own accord agree to submit unresolved disputes over interpretation of the contract to an outside party for binding decision, so that collective bargaining provides a peaceful but effective substitute for settling disputes by economic force.

Paradoxically, in any discussion of the impact of unions, it is easier to get agreement on the proposition that unions, through collective bargaining, have made a significant improvement in the lot of the employee by giving him a voice in the government of his industrial life than it is to win agreement on the *economic* consequences of unions and on the question of whether or not unions have raised wages above what they would otherwise be.

Though the discovery of the full implications of collective bargaining is often disconcerting to the businessman engaged in negotiating with a union for the first time, collective bargaining has profoundly important benefits for him as well. For by *sharing* the decision-making function with business, the American union has developed into an institution designed to compromise with the employer and to reach an agreement with him, not to get rid of him. The basic objective of the American labor movement is not to eliminate the capitalistic system, but to share in its benefits. To be sure, unions are unhesitatingly eager to win a *larger* share of those benefits, but this is quite different from wanting to replace the mechanism which provides them. Labor does not seek to kill the goose that lays the golden eggs; it wants it to lay more golden eggs, and wants more eggs for itself. Though the extravagance of their bargaining demands often obscures it, business unions are properly described as conservative—staunch defenders of the existing economic system.

Unions which are most vigorous in pressing the employers in their industry for economic gains may be just as aggressive in joining with them in seeking to protect or promote the welfare of the industry as a whole. The Teamsters Union, for example, whose energetic bargaining in the trucking industry needs no elaboration here, has been equally enthusiastic in fighting *for* the trucking industry against the inroads of "piggybacking" railroads.

A most pointed demonstration of the commitment of American labor unions to our economic system is provided by an incident occurring on a trip to Europe taken shortly after World War II by Walter Reuther, president of the United Auto Workers. Long one of the leading innovators in collective bargaining, Reuther has often been regarded uneasily by conservative members of the business community for his willingness to engage in what they regard as economic experimentation. But when Reuther toured European industry and talked with European labor leaders, he no longer played his accustomed role of business adversary and critic; instead, he was an eloquent defender of the American business system and the advantages it offered American labor. Taken through a French automobile plant by Communist union officials who bragged of their strength among French auto workers, Reuther, remarking on the bicycles lined up outside the plant, said: *"Our* members drive cars—they *buy* the products they *make*. Why should we change?"

It is often wondered, of course, how long unions can continue getting "More, now" without encroaching on profits and interfering with business incentive. The question *is* a crucial one and should not be dismissed lightly. The saving factor here is the long-run expansion of the economy and the rising productivity, which has raised real per capita income about 800 to 900 per cent in the last century. So long as this sort of economic growth prevails, *both* labor and business (and indeed, all sectors of the economy) can have "More, now" year in and year out (with due allowance for economic fluctuations). So long as the economic pie is expanding, everyone can have a larger piece simultaneously. Only if the economy were to cease growing and stagnate would we find ourselves in the situation in which labor could gain only at the expense of business or some other economic group. Then, in fact, we would be in trouble.

Their market orientation and their constant participation in the business world has made American unions remarkably business-*like* in a variety of ways. The weapons used by unions to press their demands in collective bargaining are chiefly market-oriented. The strike, the boycott, and the picket line, for example, are all market mechanisms designed to put varying degrees of pressure on the employer by cutting him off from one or another of his markets. The strike interferes with the employer's access to the labor market; the boycott, with his access to the consumer market; and the picket line, in addition to supplementing both the strike and the boycott, also impedes his access to the product market.

Relations with Other Unions

Relations between unions are also noticeably market-oriented. Like the businessman who prefers monopoly for himself and competition among his suppliers, unions are anxious to minimize the pressures of competition and to control and limit it wherever possible. As we have seen, the practice of granting each national or international union its own exclusive jurisdiction, or exclusive franchise, was designed to provide it with a monopoly over a particular occupational or industrial territory, free from competition from other unions. In fact, no more devastating charge could be made against a union than that of "dual unionism" or "rival unionism"—of competing with another union in its territory, in which it regards both workers *and* jobs as its property. Nor is this view surprising, for many charters identify both the workers and the kinds of jobs over which the union is given jurisdiction.

Problems frequently arise, however, out of the definitions of the work over which a union has jurisdiction. Many of these definitions were written many years ago and drawn to describe industrial practices of the early twentieth century. As technology has changed and industrial practices with it, what were originally distinct and separate jurisdictions now are blurred or overlapping or rendered ambiguous by changing processes and techniques.

One well-known jurisdictional dispute brought about by just such circumstances involved the Carpenters and the Sheet Metal Workers. Originally, the Carpenters jurisdictional assignment gave them control over the installation of window sash, presumably because it was made of wood, the basic criterion of whether work belonged to the Carpenters. Sheet Metal Workers, on the other hand, claimed all work having to do with sheet metal. So far, no problem. But when metal window sash was introduced, the two unions found themselves in conflict, the carpenters claiming that metal sash belonged to them because *window sash* per se was carpenter's work, while the sheet metal workers claimed it on grounds that it was now made of the *material* with which they had the exclusive right to work.

We might expect at this point that two unions, for whom collective bargaining is literally a way of life, would find a workable compromise on this problem easy to arrive at. After all, as the contractor or builder who finds himself helpless in the middle of this dispute sees it, a little reasonableness and common sense on both sides would solve the problem; if both sides give a little, everything can be taken care of.

Instead, the ensuing disputes often rivaled in intensity the bitterest labor-management conflicts. For from the viewpoint of the Carpenters and of the Sheet Metal Workers, giving a little is no more sensible or reasonable a solution than for a businessman to yield a little market to his competitor. Instead, they see the issue as setting a precedent, possibly countrywide, and not for today, but for an indefinite time in the future. If the Carpenters concede metal sash to the Sheet Metal Workers on one construction site, they may lose only a few jobs for carpenters, but multiply that a hundred times and the problem may look serious. And Carpenters Union officials are no more anxious than Churchill was to preside over the liquidation of an empire. Union officials, like members, are conscious of the scarcity of jobs; they do not cede control over *their* jobs readily. And from the Sheet Metal Workers' point of view, the problem is equally important—to fail to take advantage of expanding opportunities is to risk stagnation; it seems essential, as part of the unions' responsibility to the membership, to seize any job opportunities that come along. So what appears to the casual onlooker to be a petty argument often appears to the parties involved to be matters not merely of principle, but of institutional survival.

Disputes as to which union has the right to organize particular workers can be equally troublesome. The Retail Clerks and the Meat Cutters have fought off and on for nearly half a century without reaching any lasting agreement on the question of their respective rights to organize grocery clerks (or its counterpart, which jobs are "clerk's work"), and it is not uncommon to find the Clerks and the Meat Cutters competing for membership among grocery clerks in National Labor Relations Board elections.

Unions are not only opposed to competition between unions over members, which they regard, with some reason, as diverting energies from the main objective of improving the conditions of work; they are equally opposed to competition between workers for jobs, fearing that this kind of competition merely tends to drive down wages and aggravate an already unsatisfactory situation. Thus, it has long been a fundamental objective of union wage policy to "take wages out of competition"—to standardize wages as a means of preventing competition for jobs from driving them down. And the historic practice of limiting membership, most common in the old-line craft unions, was, whatever else may be said about it, basically a device to reduce competition for jobs and thus maintain, or raise, the price of skilled labor.

Union Finances

The business-like character of unions carries over from their behavior in the labor market into their institutional life as well. Thus, collectively, and in some cases individually, labor unions are, financially speaking, substantial organizations. As would be expected of any organization with a total of over 18 million members, large amounts of money flow in and out of union treasuries, and substantial investments are built up over the years.

A survey of the financial status of unions based on the first round of reports filed under the Landrum-Griffin Act shows that, in 1960, the total assets of the American labor movement amounted to slightly over $1.5 billion (including the assets of local unions, intermediate bodies, and national unions), while total income and total expenditures were nearly equal at $1.4 billion each.[2]

Impressive as these figures are in the aggregate, however, they indicate that union assets, as well as annual income and expenditure, average less than $100 per member. Or to put it in another perspective, *total* union assets and total union income and expenditure in 1960 were roughly comparable to the *net profits* of General Motors in 1963.

[2] *Union Financial Statistics, 1959–1960* (Washington, D.C.: Bureau of Labor-Management Reports, 1960), pp. 1–3.

And while it is popular to focus on the financial status of union giants (the Teamsters in 1960 had assets of 40 million and income of 9 million),[3] only one-fourth of all national unions had incomes of over $1 million in 1960, and one-third of all local unions reported assets of less than $2,500 and incomes and expenditures of barely $1,000 annually.[4]

Ironically, some of the practices for which business unions and their leaders are most widely criticized stem from the business ethos. The high salaries and substantial expense accounts of some top union officers, the lavish union headquarters which rival those of any business corporation, the union conventions in Miami and San Juan, the business agent's Cadillac—all this conspicuous consumption may be seen, in one perspective at least, as part of the union leaders' desire to emulate the businessmen with whom they deal, a desire to appear on equal terms with the men across the bargaining table. And if occasionally union officials misinterpret what is acceptable business conduct, what could be more flattering than to be chosen as the model of behavior, the standard for the pattern of success? In part, too, this conspicuous consumption may be the logical result of the very philosophy of business unionism, for what is it but the epitome of "More, now"?

Generally speaking, such conspicuous consumption by union leaders, far from stirring resentment or envy among the rank and file, seems to give them vicarious satisfaction; they tend to identify with their leaders and to feel that generous spending by their union is indicative of its success. They seem to say, "Look what I can afford."

Besides, the typical union member, as we shall see, is mainly interested in what the union can do for him economically. Accordingly, he tends to judge his union and his union leaders by their effect on his pocketbook. As long as his union is effective at delivering the goods, in the form of improved economic conditions, he is apt to be tolerant of its behavior in other aspects. Jimmy Hoffa's re-election to the presidency of the Teamsters Union in July 1966 (with an increase in salary from $75,000 to $100,000 a year), despite the prospects that before his term of office is over he might be jailed for jury tampering, should not be attributed simply to the effectiveness of Hoffa's skillful management of machine politics within the union, nor to a sporting insistence on the part of the members on sticking by a man when he's in trouble, although both factors were undoubtedly involved. Most observers would agree that Hoffa would win a bona fide secret-ballot election hands down, simply because the membership has made substantial economic gains during his term as Teamster president.

There are limits to the member's tolerance however, and the closer the union leader gets to understanding and imitating the businessmen with whom

---

[3] *The International Teamster* (March 1961), pp. 28–29.
[4] *Union Financial Statistics, 1959–1960, loc. cit.*

he deals, the greater the risk he runs of losing contact with his membership—a problem already grown acute in the largest unions.

The defeat of David McDonald in his bid for re-election as president of the Steelworkers, the third largest union in the country, is a pointed reminder of this fact. For, ironically enough, McDonald had more than met the traditional requirements of union leadership, economic gains of the Steelworkers during his thirteen years in office having been substantial. A frequently mentioned contributing factor in his defeat, however, was his maintenance of a residence in Palm Springs and his habit of spending long periods there, hobnobbing with Hollywood stars and leaving the running of the union in the hands of his staff. Just how important this was will never be known, but in the bitter election campaign, the picture of McDonald in his tuxedo touring the night spots of Southern California was effectively used to portray him as a man who could no longer understand the problems of the man in front of the open hearth. The problem of communication seems endemic to large organizations, regardless of their nature.

Why Workers Join Unions

When we begin to examine why workers join or fail to join unions, we find, of course, that there is not one reason, but a variety of reasons involved in their decision.

Compulsory Unionism

Today, of course, we must recognize that a substantial number of workers join unions because it is a requirement for getting or keeping the job they want. They join unions because the industry or firm where they want to work has a *union* shop in which, by union and management agreement, a worker must join the union within thirty days if he wants to keep his job, or, in the building and construction industries, a *closed* shop, in which he must belong to the union in order to be hired. By latest estimate, about 75 per cent of workers in contracts covering 1,000 or more workers each are subject to union shop provisions. The significance of this reason for union membership cannot be overlooked.

We should be careful, however, not to assume that in the absence of the compulsory-membership requirement these workers would have necessarily refrained from joining voluntarily. Some evidence of the fact that many workers would continue to join even in the absence of union-shop provisions is afforded by the recent experience in the twenty states which, since 1947, have prohibited union-shop agreements—the so-called right-to-work states. In Texas, according to Frederic Meyers, unionization began to grow rapidly in 1938 and continued to do so with "no significant diminution"[5] when that state's right-to-work law was passed in 1947.

Compulsory unionism, in fact, may be much less repugnant to the workers subject to it than it is to the public at large. In this connection, a significant experience occurred during the period 1947 to 1949, when the Taft-Hartley Act required that, before a union shop provision could be incorporated in a union-management agreement, it must be submitted to a secret-ballot vote and receive the support of a majority of those *eligible* to vote (as opposed to the customary requirement of a majority of those *voting*). Under this now defunct provision, not only was the union shop supported in 97 per cent of all these elections, but, of over 4 million workers voting in them, over 94 per cent voted in favor.[6] These overwhelming majorities in favor of the union shop, in fact, led Senator Taft, one of the sponsors of the Taft-Hartley Act, to urge successfully the dropping of the union shop election provision on the grounds that the record indicated that it was a waste of the government's time and effort to put the question to a vote. As it now stands, therefore, the question whether the union shop is to become a part of a labor-management agreement is simply a matter of bargaining between the representatives of the parties.

Voluntary Unionism

Since neither the union shop nor the closed shop is possible until a union has been formed, has been recognized by an employer, and has negotiated a contract, let us return to the basic questions of why workers join voluntarily and why they form unions in the first place. Many theories have been advanced to explain workers' decisions when they are free to choose whether or not to join a union. The basic element in that decision can be stated quite simply: the worker will choose to join a union if and when he thinks it pays off in terms of his economic welfare or his status among his friends and associates. The problem, therefore, is to distinguish the types of workers or the circumstances which fit these requirements.

The unskilled It is often supposed that the first workers to turn to unions as a solution to their problems were those who were economically the most depressed and exploited and whose working conditions most obviously called for improvement—namely, the unskilled workers. Such conditions may well have generated a strong *motivation* toward joining unions, but if so, such motivation was not sufficient. Successful unionization requires *both* motiva-

[5] Frederic Meyers, "Effects of 'Right-to-Work' Laws: A Study of the Texas Act," *Industrial and Labor Relations Review* (October 1955), p. 78.
[6] Fred Witney, *Government and Collective Bargaining* (Philadelphia: Lippincott, 1951), p. 341.

tion and economic leverage or bargaining power. Because the unskilled were readily replaceable, strikes or threats of strikes were probably more risky for the workers than for their employers. In short, their decision to quit or strike caused little hardship for their employers; they had no bargaining power—and unions without bargaining power do not pay off. Consequently, it has only been most recently, under special and unusual circumstances, that unskilled workers have been able to unionize successfully.

The skilled   Thus, the first workers to unionize, in the United States as well as in Britain, were not the most downtrodden or the lowest paid. Far from it; unions first appeared among the economic elite of the working class, those whose wages were the highest and working conditions the best—the skilled workers, who had *both* motivation for organizing *and* the leverage to make the organization effective.

The skilled workers' initial motivation for organizing was originally less a desire to win "More, now" than a desire to protect the superior (for that period) economic position they already possessed from being undermined by competition from cheap labor. It is not accidental that many of the early unions called themselves "protective associations."

The competition which threatened the skilled workers took a variety of forms. In some cases, it was the arrival of new waves of immigrants, adding to the labor supply, with the predictable economic consequence that their availability tended to drive down the price of labor—that is, wages. And it was not simply that employers were willing to substitute new unskilled labor for their skilled employees, for the immigrants included skilled labor as well as unskilled. But the immigrants were often ignorant of local market conditions and, being used to the generally lower wages of countries from which they had come, were willing to work for wages lower than prevailed here. In such a case, those already employed might be confronted with the choice of taking wage cuts or being replaced.

More often, however, the competition came from lower-priced products made by lower-paid workers and sold in the market in competition with the products made by the skilled workers. Under these conditions, the employer found that, unless he met the price of competing products, his sales would drop and employment with them; this in turn led him to seek to cut his labor costs as a way of preserving his profits in the face of price competition. And again, the high-wage employee faced the threat of loss of employment due to low-wage competition unless he could secure a uniform wage standard among all competitors.

Equally important was the fact that their skill gave these workers bargaining power. Unlike the unskilled worker, who could be quickly replaced, the craftsmen of the early eighteenth century could impose a real hardship on employers by striking. Their period of apprentice training was a long one, and the supply of men in any skilled craft was relatively small. Accordingly, they were hard to replace, particularly if numbers of them ceased work simultaneously. And rather than face the consequences of trying to find replacements, employers frequently found it preferable to accede to the demands of the skilled workers and their organizations.

Unions first appeared among skilled workers, then, when these workers were motivated to protect their position and because their market position gave them the bargaining power necessary to make unions pay off effectively.

Undoubtedly the best known description of the *general* circumstances under which unions would meet the economic and social needs of workers is that of the late Professor Perlman of the University of Wisconsin.[7] His theory is that the American worker turned to unions only when he had concluded that he was not going to "get ahead" by moving up into the managerial ranks or by becoming self-employed. So long as he seriously entertained such hopes, joining a union was not the answer to his objectives, but was a tacit admission that he had abandoned them, an open recognition that he had given up the American dream of poor boy makes good. But whenever the worker recognized that the odds were heavily weighted against his getting a higher pay-off in this way, it became logical to turn to methods which would maximize the economic gains to be had *as employee*—in short, to join a union.

On the other hand, to those who look forward to moving into the managerial or supervisory ranks (white-collar workers, for example), or who expect to become self-employed, the probable pay-off from their individual advancement is likely to be greater than that offered by union membership.

Even the current union activity among such professional groups as teachers, nurses, doctors, and even priests (see Chapter 1), though it does not match the *details* of this theory, is consistent with its *basic* point—namely, that the decision to join or not to join a union is, among other things, an economic one.

Similarly, those who work part-time, or expect to be employed only a short time, such as young women who regard a job as a hopefully brief interlude between school and marriage, are likely to see little economic reason for joining a union; the costs loom large, and the anticipated benefits to be gained in the course of short-run or part-time employment seem small. In these circumstances, their attitude tends to be: "I'm not going to be here long. Why should I join?"

Status

Another variable in the equation is status. It is often argued that the white-collar worker's demonstrated reluctance to join unions is due to a fear

[7] Selig Perlman, *A Theory of the Labor Movement* (New York: Macmillan, 1928), p. 321.

of losing status—to a feeling that unions are for blue-collar workers only. Since this attitude has persisted long after the average weekly earnings of blue-collar workers moved above those of nonsupervisory white-collar workers, we must conclude that white-collar workers are willing to make economic sacrifices to maintain their status.

Perhaps what is really behind the status factor is the problem of conformity. Most of us, whether at home or at work, tend to conform and find it easier and more comfortable to follow the practices and behavior of the majority. For this very reason, both union strength and union weakness tend to be self-reinforcing.

If a union has already achieved success in a community, is well established, numerically strong, and accepted, the new employee is likely to see membership as part of the prevailing pattern and to join, if only to do as the Romans do. If the union includes only a small minority, as is still the case for most white-collar unions, membership tags one as part of that minority; thus, belonging is nonconforming behavior, and the typical reaction is to avoid it. The union problem in this case, of course, is how to make the transition from minority to majority status.

The Business Cycle and Union Growth

The priority given to economic performance by both unions and workers alike suggests that union membership will tend to fluctuate in accordance with the economic achievements of unions—with their success in getting "More, now" through collective bargaining.

Obviously, economic conditions are among the vital factors affecting a union's economic performance. Let us see, then, how fluctuations in economic activity affect union activity and union membership. Let us see the relationship between the growth of market-oriented business unions and the business cycle.

It is often supposed that union membership behaves counter-cyclically, with membership expanding in depression and falling off or stabilizing during boom. The reasoning behind this analysis is obvious—it assumes that poverty and depression and the fear of unemployment (if not the actual experience of it) are just the economic circumstances which turn people to unions, in a desperate effort to remedy their situation. And conversely, this line of reasoning leads to the conclusion that, during prosperous times, when jobs are plentiful and wages good, workers will see nothing to be gained by joining unions and union membership will level off or decline.

On the face of it, this argument is plausible enough. And the fact that the great union expansion of the 1930's began during the worst depression the United States ever weathered lends it impressive support.

But reality is almost the direct opposite of this. With certain interesting exceptions, such as that noted above (which can be explained in part as an *aftermath* of depression), union membership tends generally to move *with* rather than counter to the business cycle; it tends to rise in prosperity and fall in depression. The reason? Prosperity gives the union its most favorable opportunity for effective union performance, its best chance to pay off for the members.

In other words, to paraphrase a well-known chestnut, "What's good for General Motors is good for organized labor." And this is literally, as well as figuratively, true. For in 1965, while General Motors (and the rest of the auto industry) reached record levels of production and profits, the United Auto Workers gained over 150,000 members. What better measure could we have of the *mutual* interests of market-oriented unions and business firms?

This comes about for a number of reasons. The relative scarcity of workers and the relative plenty of jobs characteristic of prosperity give unions extra bargaining power—a seller's market for labor, in other words. This not only enables a union to press for greater gains than usual, but increases their probability of winning them as well. The existence of the seller's market also makes the threat of a strike more serious, for replacing strikers becomes more difficult. And finally, when there is a seller's market for labor, there will be a seller's market for the goods and services of their employer. (In fact, the causal relationship runs the other way; the demand for labor is derived from the demand for the employer's product.) Far from making the employer more adamant in his bargaining, these circumstances tend to make him more willing to compromise. First, he is likely to be in a better financial position to meet the union's demands (that is, better able to *afford* bigger concessions than at any other time during the cycle), and second, he is anxious to maintain production and will accept fairly high costs rather than see it interrupted. Although as a result of the superior earnings that come with prosperity he is better equipped than usual to engage in a protracted struggle with the union, if he is in a competitive industry, he is likely to put a very high priority on maintaining production without interruption. Perhaps nothing will bring an employer to terms more rapidly than to see his competitor in full operation while his own plant is shut down by a strike. For this means that the competitor is not only making money while the strike-bound employer is shut down, but that he is, in all likelihood, also capturing customers who may never return. For these reasons, then, the employer's willingness to settle in order to avoid a strike, and the union's ability to make economic gains, tend to be at a peak, rather than a low, during prosperity.

This point is most clearly made by Leland Hazard, former Vice-president and General Counsel of the Pittsburgh Plate Glass Company, when he says:

> The factors which move the more influential segments of industrial management to a wage decision are: (1) the compulsion to maintain production, (2)

the need to maintain a feasible price, and (3) the *sine qua non* profit . . . Production, price and profit—*And the greatest of these is production.*[8]

. . . A customer (big and scarce) lost for lack of production is a loss the finality of which impresses management more than the immediate inability to increase a price to reflect a wage increase, and more than the threat that wages will presently absorb too much of profits. The time will come when the price *can* be increased, the engineers will find a way . . . to increase the productivity to offset the wage. But a lost customer—that sad event—leaves a manager inconsolable.[9]

. . . It is obvious that the compulsion to maintain uninterrupted production will be a more potent factor in wage determination on the upswing of the business cycle than on the downswing . . . on the nether side (downswing) of the cycle an interruption will be less devastating to a customer . . . because alternative sources of supply are available.[10]

And conversely, during depression or recession the combination of a buyer's market for labor with its attendant advantage to the employer; the likelihood that facilities are not being fully utilized anyhow; and the facts that interruption of production is not likely to inconvenience a customer who is not ordering anyhow, that there is little economic fat to give to the union, and that workers who realize that they may be readily replaced by unemployed workers are less likely to risk strike action than ones who are confident of the difficulty of finding replacements—all combine to make periods of depressed economic activity difficult ones in which to improve the worker's economic lot, through collective bargaining or otherwise.

Thus, we find ourselves faced with the fact that a union's ability to deliver the goods, economically speaking, and its ability to reach prospective members where it counts—in the pocketbook—are directly affected by economic conditions.

And though it is doubtless true that the workers' economic position will improve during prosperity whether they are unionized or not, there is at least some significant evidence that members of the biggest and/or most powerful unions get gains above and beyond those of nonunion workers. In any case, unions tend to take the credit for improvements accruing to workers, and to the extent that this is accepted by employees, successful negotiations are perhaps the best organizing appeal there is.

The theory which we have been developing here gets substantial support when we look at the actual history of changes in union membership.

No better demonstration could be given than the experience of American unions since 1961. Under the stimulus of an expanding economy and virtual

---

[8] Leland Hazard, "Wage Theory: A Management View," in George W. Taylor and Frank C. Pierson, eds., *New Concepts in Wage Determination* (New York: McGraw-Hill, 1957), p. 32.
[9] *Ibid.,* p. 45.
[10] *Ibid.,* p. 48.

boom conditions, employment in the manufacturing industries and the blue-collar occupations rose, carrying union membership figures up with it, if only because a large proportion of union contracts in the manufacturing industries contain a union-shop provision. While it may be that there is a qualitative difference between such automatic membership and membership acquired through organizing drives (presently more typical in the service industries), it makes no difference in the statistics of union membership: the recovery of union membership in manufacturing has been probably the most important single factor in the rise of total union membership in the past three years.

Of late, still another factor has exerted a positive influence in terms of union growth—the war in Vietnam. Unpleasant as it may seem, one of the effects of such a war is economic expansion—in short, a war boom, which, like any other economic expansion, tends to be beneficial to both industry and labor.

Communist Union Growth

In a predominately market-oriented labor movement such as we have in the United States, unions with a primarily ideological or political orientation, such as Communist-dominated unions, tend to have a distinctive appeal largely for those who are dissatisfied with the operation of the economic system and want to replace it with something else rather than work within the existing framework. So far as economic circumstances contribute toward receptiveness to such views, one would expect that the left-wing unions would attract the largest number of followers in times of economic depression, when the tangible rewards of our economic system are at a minimum, and the smallest numbers in periods of prosperity. To put it another way, one would expect membership in Communist-dominated unions to move in the opposite direction from the business cycle (in a counter-cyclical pattern), rather than to follow it as membership in the business unions tends to.

The experience of Communist-dominated unions in the past thirty-five years or so substantially confirms this view. The depression of the 1930's, which at its depth found 25 per cent of the labor force unemployed, many not just for months, but for years, was a period of intense activity on the part of Communists in the labor movement. And by the end of World War II, they had reached a peak strength, aided by the unusual circumstance of the United States' wartime alliance with Russia.

But the postwar prosperity has apparently had a detrimental impact on Communist influence in the labor movement. After more than twenty years of unparalleled prosperity and rising real incomes, few workers want to replace the system that produced it with something else. While no accurate figures are available on the membership of either the Communist Party in the United States or its strength among union members, it seems hardly coincidental that during this period the *Daily Worker,* the official newspaper of the Communists, was forced by dwindling sales to change to *The Worker* (bi-weekly), and that of some eleven unions expelled from the CIO in 1949–50 on grounds of Communist domination, only four were left as separate unions by 1955.

Indeed, it appears that, to survive, the Communist-dominated unions have been forced, for tactical reasons, to compete on the business unions' own terms of delivering the goods—economically speaking.

The Economics of Organizing

Whether or not workers join unions depends on two types of factors—those which affect the willingness of workers to join unions and those which affect the organizing activity of the unions themselves. For while it is true that many of the elements that affect the workers' willingness to join unions are beyond the control of the unions, it is also true that it is not enough simply for workers to be favorably disposed toward unions. New members are more often acquired through organizing campaigns than from would-be members knocking at the union door. Unions are well aware that salesmanship is often necessary to convert a potential customer into an active one, and substantial resources, both in time and money, go into organizing campaigns.

An example of this may be seen in the 1965 AFL-CIO Executive Council Report, which notes that in the two-year period July 1, 1963, to June 30, 1965, a special organizing drive to enlist new members in the Los Angeles-Orange County area had required total expenditures of over $300,000 and produced "well over 60,000 new members," at a unit cost of about $5 per new member.[11]

Similarly, the Teamsters Union reported that for the year ending December 31, 1965, organizing campaigns had cost some $2.5 million (exclusive of organizers' salaries and expenses), an amount which represented 15 per cent of the total operating expenses of the international union;[12] and this figure gives no idea of how much more was spent by local unions on the same organizing drives. And yet for this expense, total membership in the Teamsters Union is reported to have increased by only 47,000 members. Here, net cost of a "permanent" addition to membership ran in the vicinity of $60 per capita, a much greater cost than that of the AFL-CIO campaign reported above.

Since organizing is an expensive process that draws heavily on a union's financial and manpower resources, it tries to utilize them economically and

[11] *Report of the AFL-CIO Executive Council,* Sixth Convention, San Francisco, 1965, p. 58.
[12] *The International Teamster* (March 1966), p. 28.

to spend them where they will do the most good. This means deciding *which* workers are the critical ones to win over to the union cause.

As we have seen, "Labor organization emerges among employees who have strategic market or technological positions. They have bargaining power. They can make it hurt. These strategic employees may be regarded as 'points of infection' or 'growth cones' . . . for the spread of labor organization."[13] In organizing a plant or store, therefore, a union doesn't pay equal attention to all workers, but tries to concentrate its energies where they will be most effective. In retail trades, for example, crucial occupations *within* the store have been the meat-cutters (in supermarkets) or shoe clerks, or appliance salesmen (in department stores). In the clothing industries, the cutters were the first to be organized.

In each case, the crucial occupations have been the first to be organized because they had a skill that was hard to replace, and accordingly, had substantial bargaining power. They had status—their skill, bargaining power, and superior earnings lead other workers to look up to and respect them; when they join the union, they set an example for others to follow. In short, the skilled and strategically located worker is *still* the first to be organized, just as he was a century and a half ago.

In any discussion of union organizing tactics, it should be recognized that, historically at least, persuading *workers* that they should join the union was only one of the methods of organizing unions. Many unions in the past have found it both quicker and less expensive to focus their energies on persuading the *employer* to recognize the union—without consulting the employees directly involved; hence, the so-called "sweetheart agreement," bitterly criticized as undemocratic, in which the union induced the employer to recognize it directly as representative of his employees, with the result that the new members often learned of their membership by an announcement from the employer. In such cases, the union may seek help from such strategic workers as the teamsters, who may not be employed at the plant or store being organized, but simply may handle its deliveries. In this case, the organizer's tactics may involve persuading teamsters to come to his assistance by exerting pressure on the employer to recognize the union as representative of his workers.[14]

There are other variables that affect the costs of organizing. Such factors as high labor turnover or the scattering of workers among many employers or over wide geographic areas can impede union growth by causing high per capita organizing costs.

---

[13] John T. Dunlop, "The Development of Labor Organization: A Theoretical Framework," in Richard A. Lester and Joseph Shister, eds., *Insights into Labor Issues* (New York: Macmillan, 1948), p. 180.

[14] See Marten S. Estey, "The Strategic Alliance as a Factor in Union Growth," *Industrial and Labor Relations Review,* October 1955, pp. 41–53.

High labor turnover is expensive for unions because it forces them, in the absence of a union shop or closed shop, to organize two or three workers to maintain a single membership. One of the great advantages to the union of compulsory union membership lies in the fact that it is such an efficient and inexpensive organizing device. And where a union is trying to organize industries characterized by many small and widely scattered plants, an organizer may have to visit many plants just to contact a few hundred workers. Instead of meeting with large groups of workers, the organizer may have to recruit workers almost individually, with the result that his productivity is low and organizing costs are high.

Unfortunately for the unions, both high labor turnover and wide dispersal of labor are characteristic of the service industries, in which the principal expansion of the labor force is occurring. Added to the problem of worker indifference or hostility to them, unions are faced with the hard fact that the major unorganized sectors of the economy are inherently costly to organize. So far as organizing is concerned, the rich veins have already been tapped, the cream has been skimmed off the top, and only the high-cost reserves remain.

Motivation for Organizing

But the union decision to invest in an organizing drive is more than a matter of weighing the costs of organizing against the probable future revenue to be obtained from the new member; it is more than a question of imperialistic motives, the desire to expand simply for expansion's sake. Thus, while there is doubtless an important element of empire-building in the organizing activities of any union (as well as an element of the old-fashioned missionary bringing the gospel to the heathen), the motivation of union organizing drives cannot be properly appreciated if we ignore the fact that one of the most urgent and persistent pressures on unions to expand membership is the presence, in a partially organized industry, of nonunion firms which act as an obstacle to the improvement of the wages, hours, and working conditions of union men.

So long as there are nonunion firms in an industry, the improvement of union wages tends to create a differential within the industry which works to the competitive disadvantage of the unionized employer. Eventually he reaches a point at which the differential is more than he can absorb or offset, and his resistance to further gains is stiffened and/or he is threatened by a loss of business to his lower-cost competitors. In either case, the union is hurt. Accordingly, the union is under continuous pressure, quite aside from any imperialistic motives, to organize nonunion firms to remove the barrier to bargaining gains for their present members. And since economic gains may be the *sine qua non* for holding their existing membership, expansion may, in some cases, be almost literally a matter of institutional survival. Under such circumstances, the union may look on the nonunion worker not simply as a prospective customer to be wooed by effective salesmanship, but also as an unethical competitor who is jeopardizing the welfare of the union. With such a view, the democratic right of the nonunion worker to join or not is easily lost sight of, as the union resorts to any method available to it to rid itself of competition.

This pressure, which is of fundamental importance in constantly pushing unions toward expanding their scope in private business and industry, may be significantly diminished, if not altogether lacking, when it comes to union activity in the public sector or in the private but nonprofit sector of the economy.

Consider the case of laundry workers in hospitals. Hospital laundry workers have long been noted for receiving lower wages than their counterparts in commercial laundries. Regardless of the argument occasionally advanced that there are offsetting advantages, in the form of less onerous working conditions and a less demanding pace, a key reason for the long indifference of the laundry unions to the plight of the hospital laundrymen is the simple fact that hospital laundries are basically not in competition with commercial laundries—their low wages and presumably low costs do not threaten to intrude into or encroach upon the market of the commercial laundries. Hospital laundries do not threaten to seize a share of the commercial laundries' business. And accordingly, unionized employees of commercial laundries are under no *economic* pressure to bring the hospital employees into the fold. A major force for unionization is thus missing.

The same is true of other employees in hospitals, universities, and other nonprofit institutions, and in that far larger group, the government employees. In no case are they really competing for the business done by industrial and commercial counterparts; and since they are no threat to the welfare of the industrial or commercial worker, there is no pressing need for unions in industry to bring them up to industrial and commercial levels.

Teamsters Union Growth—A Case in Point

This analysis of the factors which influence workers to join unions is helpful not only in understanding over-all trends in union membership, but also in shedding light on the trends of union membership in particular industries. We have seen, for example, that the Teamsters Union in the past decade has gained more members than any other union, despite a continuous storm of controversy about its leadership. A brief look at the environment in which the Teamsters operate suggests that there are sound objective reasons for their leading position as a growth union.

The Teamsters deal, first of all, with a segment of the labor force which seems likely to find unionism attractive. In their basic jurisdiction in the trucking industry, the proportion of workers who consider themselves permanently in the employee category is fairly high; opportunities for self-employment, while still an important factor in trucking, appear to be declining as costs of equipment rise. There are few women and relatively few white-collar workers—few of the workers for whom unions tend to be a questionable investment.

At the same time, economic factors are favorable to Teamster growth. Their bargaining power is unquestionable. The economic leverage and bargaining power flowing from their strategic position is almost unrivaled. Because a large and increasing proportion of all goods is moved to and from the factory or store by truck, the Teamsters control a strategic bottleneck, with which they can inflict great costs on an employer at little cost to themselves.

They are in an expanding industry, with all the economic advantages that entails. In addition, to take the greatest possible advantage of economic growth of the trucking industry and to overcome the adverse effects of non-union competition, the union, through Hoffa, has been moving for several years toward national collective bargaining for intercity freight and other segments of the Teamsters jurisdiction.

Furthermore, in a period when the Steelworkers and the Auto Workers (the former in particular) were under great pressure from the White House to confine their bargaining gains to the 3.4 per cent per year limits imposed by the Council of Economic Advisers wage guidelines, the Teamsters, a large part of whose bargaining is still conducted at the local level rather than at the national union level (unlike either the Steelworkers or the Auto Workers), were demanding and getting settlements well in excess of the guidelines. They did this with impunity, well aware that the guidelines can be effectively enforced only in a situation in which national bargaining is practiced. Accordingly, while the Steelworkers, in particular, were having to content themselves with rather moderate gains, the Teamsters were able, by virtue of the widely dispersed character of the trucking industry, to take a much more aggressive stance.

The collective impact of these factors is almost entirely favorable—a labor force which includes relatively few groups resistant to unions, ample bargaining power and economic leverage, and the stimulus of economic growth in the industry—with all that implies concerning satisfactory performance by the union.

6

The State and the Unions

This chapter deals with what is commonly referred to as public policy with regard to union activity. Public policy is not a synonym for public opinion about labor issues, although it is often influenced by it. Public policy refers to *government* policy with respect to unions and their behavior.

Public policy in the field of labor is expressed in a variety of ways—in law, in administrative rulings and interpretations, in "guidelines," and even in decisions as to how and when to intervene in particular disputes or problems.

In the present chapter, we have confined our attention to the most basic expression of public policy, the law. The law provides the general ground rules of the game for unions and for union-management relations; it establishes the general boundaries between proper and improper conduct. And as in other games, the rules are constantly evolving and being re-evaluated.

But despite the dynamic nature of public policy, it is important to realize the extent to which the basic issues involved in public policy persist. While the problems with which public policy deals vary unceasingly, these variations are often simply different manifestations of an historic issue. Questions such as how to balance the conflicting rights of nonunion workers, union members, and the public at large; what methods unions should be permitted in pursuing their objectives; and even where to draw the line between public and private determination of labor relations problems are among the persistent and recurring issues of public policy which have been with us since the Cordwainer's case in 1806 and for which new answers have to be found as new developments occur.

Although the development of public policy for labor relations appears here as a number of discrete events, each occurring at a particular time and place, it would be a mistake to assume that each turn of policy, each major court decision, and each major piece of legislation was simply a response to the circumstances and pressures of the moment. A more realistic and useful view is that each of these events represents the culmination of a long period of concern and experimentation and that the development of public policy is a continuous process of evolution and adaptation to changing economic and social facts and needs.

Common versus Statute Law

In the United States, the law of labor relations has been expressed over the years in two basic forms, common law and statute law. American common law, which is an outgrowth of the English legal system, is sometimes referred to as unwritten law because it is in part based on custom and precedent. In general, however, it is more accurate to think of common law as judge-made law, consisting of court decisions interpreting existing laws or deciding issues not yet subject to statute law. In any case, the volumes of court decisions in the nearest law library are mute evidence that common law is amply documented.

In contrast to common law, statute law is law enacted by legislative bodies and expressed in a formal document. It includes the laws passed by the Congress of the United States and those passed by the various state legislatures, though we will be primarily concerned here with Federal rather than state legislation.

One widely held view is that in the field of social policy, including union activity and labor relations, the common law has tended to be more conservative and less adaptable to changing economic and social conditions than statute law, both in England and in the United States. And certainly, as we look at the development of American public policy towards unions, it is apparent that, broadly speaking, so long as public policy was shaped primarily by the courts, say from 1800 to the 1920's, it was generally restrictive and restraining, while since the 1920's, it has been predominantly expressed in statute law and has been generally unrestrictive and encouraging. To explain this dichotomy it is generally noted that legislative bodies, being composed of elected officials, are more likely to reflect and be sensitive to public opinion than are the courts, whose officials are generally appointed, and that by the very nature of its functions, the legislative branch of government is bound to be more innovative than the judicial branch.

But perhaps the more fundamental reason for the shift in the 1920's from a restrictive to an encouraging legal climate for unions is to be found in the long-term shifts in the composition of the labor force. During most of the nineteenth century, we were still predominantly an agricultural society. More than half the population was still on farms or in small towns, and was traditionally anticollectivist and antiunion. By 1920, a great migration from the farm to the factory and from the country to the city had taken place, climaxed by the impetus given it by World War I. The voting population had become a predominantly urban and industrial one, with the problems, interests, and outlook of industrial workers and urbanites. *This,* in the last analysis, is what underlies the shift in public policy; this explains the timing of that shift.

The Conspiracy Doctrine

Thirty years after the Declaration of Independence, another historic event took place in Philadelphia—the first American court case involving the right of workers to belong to unions, engage in collective bargaining, and resort to economic action to gain their objectives. But the decision of the court in this case—the Philadelphia Cordwainers (shoemakers) Case of 1806—was no declaration of independence for the industrial worker; ironically enough the outcome was just the opposite, for the court, depending on English common law, which from the middle of the fourteenth century had treated as illegal all attempts to raise wages by "concerted" (i.e., organized) action, noted that "a combination of workmen to raise their wages may be considered in a twofold point of view; one is to benefit themselves . . . the other to injure those who do not join their society. The rule of the law condemns both," and proceeded to find the cordwainers guilty of conspiracy.[1]

This did not mean, of course, that it was illegal for the individual workman to seek a wage increase; what was illegal, and what constituted the conspiracy, was the mere fact of *collective* action—quite irrespective of the facts that the objective of higher wages was itself legal and that no methods unlawful *per se* were used.

The hard line taken in the Cordwainers case was subsequently eased in the case of Commonwealth v. Hunt in 1842, when what would now be called the rule of reason was applied to union activity. Here the judge ruled that, for a union to be guilty of conspiracy, either its objective or the means used

[1] Fred Witney, *Government and Collective Bargaining* (Philadelphia: Lippincott, 1951), p. 29.

to reach it must be criminal or unlawful. Thus, the court no longer regarded unions as necessarily synonymous with conspiracy, but acknowledged that they might have beneficial as well as adverse public impact.

Seen in retrospect, the Cordwainers case is perhaps of chiefly symbolic interest (although the charge of conspiracy continued to be a significant issue in court cases involving labor until the 1880's). Quite apart from its specific content, it is significant as the case that ushered in what we describe here as the common-law era of public policy toward organized labor and set the essentially restrictive tone which was to prevail, with variations and modifications, for more than a century.

Equally important is the fact that the Cordwainers case presents in microcosm the fundamental issues with respect to the rights of workers and unions with which the makers of public policy have grappled from that day to this. Thus, while their specific manifestations (and the policy positions related to them) have changed, the basic issues—of the proper balance between property rights and human rights, between the rights and freedoms of union members and those of nonunion workers, and between the rights of the worker to organize and bargain collectively and the rights of the public at large—are as crucial today as they were one hundred and sixty years ago. The Cordwainers case is a vivid reminder that it is not so much the problems and issues that change, as our concepts of them and our views as to how they should be dealt with.

The Injunction

As the conspiracy doctrine dwindled in importance, unions found themselves confronted with another legal obstacle—the injunction, or court order to cease and desist from some specified action such as a strike, a boycott, or picketing. Violation of the order, of course, is contempt of court and punishable accordingly; this is what put the teeth into the injunction.

In labor relations, as in other uses, the injunction is primarily a preventive device, developed to cope with the fact that in many situations, damages or losses resulting from certain actions cannot be adequately compensated for, either because what is damaged or destroyed cannot be replaced, or because the dollar value of the loss cannot be properly calculated. If a hundred-year-old tree in front of your house is about to be cut down by the city in a street widening program, an injunction (if you can get it) is clearly preferable to trying to replace the tree after it is cut down, or trying to estimate its dollar value. Similarly, employers have turned to the courts for injunctions against strikes, picketing, and boycotts on the grounds that these union activities threatened to cause irreparable or incalculable damage, not necessarily to their physical property, but more generally to their property right to do business and make profits.

In the United States, the use of the injunction in labor disputes began in the 1880's, when they were issued by a number of state courts. The labor injunction received its greatest impetus, however, in 1894, when the Federal government obtained an injunction to end the famous Pullman strike and was upheld by the Supreme Court in its contention that the injunction was a legitimate measure for the control of labor disputes. After this decision, the use of the labor injunction became widespread and continued so for nearly forty years, until the passage of the Norris-LaGuardia Act in 1932.

The injunction was an effective way of controlling unions, for by preventing strikes, picketing, and boycotts, and thus restricting or depriving unions of the use of their principal economic weapons, it severely limited their power and effectiveness in collective bargaining. Union leaders accordingly viewed the injunction with particular distaste, maintaining that "no weapon has been used with such disastrous effects against trade unions as has the injunction."[2] One impartial authority has concluded that from the 1890's to the 1930's the injunction was used "to assist in defeating most of the more important strikes . . . to prevent the successful spreading of labor boycotts . . . and . . . to prevent organizing activities."[3]

Aside from its impact on unions, an important aspect of the widespread use of the injunction during this period was that it put the courts increasingly into a central role in labor disputes and further enhanced their part in determining public policy in *practice*—a fact which led to bitter union complaints of "government by injunction."

Increasing doubts about the wisdom of such extensive judicial intervention in labor disputes (to say nothing of questions as to judicial impartiality or lack of it), plus concern over an apparent trend toward increasingly restrictive injunctions and the granting of temporary injunctions without benefit of hearings, eventually led to the Norris-LaGuardia Act of 1932, which imposed substantial restrictions on their use and effectively reduced the role of the Federal courts in labor disputes.

While the use of the injunction was in some degree restored when the Taft-Hartley Act made it available for use by the Federal government, and while the Norris-LaGuardia Act does not control the issuance of injunctions by state courts, the fact remains that since Norris-LaGuardia, the injunction has been of limited significance in labor disputes in interstate commerce.

Antitrust Law

Almost at the same time that the injunction was being turned into a device for curbing union power, another, though probably less effective, restraint

---

[2] John Mitchell, former president of the United Mine Workers, as quoted in Harry A. Millis and Royal E. Montgomery, *Organized Labor* (New York: McGraw-Hill, 1945), p. 631.
[3] *Loc. cit.*

on the unions' use of economic measures was developed when the courts, by interpretation, extended the application of the antitrust laws from business firms—for which they were presumably designed—to unions.

The original Federal antitrust law, of course, was the Sherman Antitrust Act of 1890, which prohibits both "combinations in restraint of trade" and "attempts to monopolize trade" and provides that offenders shall be punished by fine or imprisonment or both and be subject to triple damages. Unlike the injunction, the Sherman Act is not preventive. Its effectiveness lies in the prospects that punishments after the fact will discourage future violations, but it is obviously a less direct restraint on union action than the injunction.

Although a number of lower courts had already applied the Sherman Act to unions, the key decision so far as organized labor was concerned was that of the Supreme Court in the Danbury Hatters case (*Loewe* v. *Lawlor*) in 1908. During the course of an organizing campaign at the Loewe Hat Company, the United Hatters union had applied economic pressure on the company by persuading the American Federation of Labor to urge union members throughout the country to refrain from buying Loewe's hats—in short, to boycott the company. The question before the Court was whether this boycott, which had been followed by a decline in the company's interstate sales, constituted a restraint of trade prohibited by the Sherman Act. The Supreme Court ruled that the boycott *was* a violation of the Act and thus opened the way to the use of the Sherman Act against labor's major economic weapon, the strike (although, in fact, there was no major case of a strike being found in violation of the Sherman Act until the 1920's).

Shortly after the Danbury Hatters decision, the Sherman Act was amended by the passage of the Clayton Act of 1914, Section 6 of which specified, among other things, that "Nothing contained in the anti-trust laws shall be construed to forbid the existence and operation of labor . . . organizations . . . nor shall such organizations or the members thereof, be held or construed to be illegal combinations or conspiracies in restraint of trade, under the anti-trust laws."[4] Union leaders were elated, for they believed that Section 6 clearly and unmistakably removed them from the restrictions of the Sherman Act and left them free once more to use their economic weapons without fear of legal action. Indeed, Samuel Gompers himself hailed the Clayton Act as an "Industrial Magna Charta."

Labor's elation, however, proved short-lived. For when the Clayton Act was tested in the courts, the judicial interpretation was that Section 6 had not changed the fundamental fact that it was the *activities* of a union that determined whether or not it was in violation of the antitrust law. The duplex Printing case, in 1921, which paralleled Danbury Hatters to the extent of involving the same economic weapon, the secondary boycott, offered an ideal test case of the Clayton Act. And the Supreme Court, as in the earlier case,

---

[4] Witney, *op. cit.,* pp. 637–638.

found that the *action* violated the Sherman Act. In short, nothing had been changed by the Clayton Act; in terms of the antitrust laws, unions were back where they had been in 1908, when the Danbury Hatters decision was rendered.

Indeed, they were worse off, for between the Danbury and Duplex decisions, the Federal courts, at least, had applied the antitrust laws only to secondary boycotts and to strikes in a single industry, the railroads. After Duplex, however, the Supreme Court found strikes in manufacturing and in coal mining also to be in restraint of trade.

So far as the Sherman Act was concerned, labor's real Magna Charta came in 1940 and 1941, when the long record of judicial decisions placing unions under the restrictions of the antitrust laws was reversed in three key cases, the Apex case, the Milk-Wagon Drivers case, and the Hutcheson case. All legal technicalities aside, the basic fact is that in these three cases, the Supreme Court held that, even where they reduced the flow of goods in interstate commerce, strikes, boycotts, and picketing no longer violated the antitrust laws if the restraint of trade was an *incidental* consequence of the union's pursuit of its primary objective of winning a labor dispute. Unions thus found themselves virtually free to use their economic weapons with impunity. Only in the case of collusion, where a union together with an employer acted to restrain trade or monopolize an industry, was union activity *per se* still subject to the antitrust laws.

Though these key decisions were handed down over a quarter of a century ago, in the first bloom of the New Deal, they stand unchanged as the law of the land so far as the application of the antitrust laws to organized labor is concerned. And although nearly every major strike brings out a rash of proposals to bring unions under the antitrust laws again and complaints against their privileged status with respect to them, it seems likely that this could come about only if specific legislation were enacted amending the Norris-LaGuardia Act and returning labor policy to its pre-1930 stance; short of such legislative changes, it seems unlikely that court interpretations alone will significantly change the tenor of public policy in this regard.

Railway Labor Act

The transition from common law to statute law as the chief instrument of public policy with respect to unions and collective bargaining was, of course, a long, drawn-out process, reflecting both the changing economic and social structure and the many preliminary experiments and attempts at statute law. It is convenient, nevertheless, to resort to a sort of historical shorthand and use some particular event or date to mark the turning point when common law was superseded by statute law as the primary source of public labor policy. With these qualifications, the appropriate turning point is the Railway Labor Act of 1926, which, although not the first Federal statute to deal with the rights of workers to join unions, was historic because it was the first of its kind to pass the scrutiny of the Supreme Court.

The Railway Labor Act may be viewed both as an end and a beginning. With its own antecedents in such earlier experiments in Federal protection of union activity as the Erdman Act of 1898 (declared unconstitutional in 1908) and the National War Labor Board of 1918 (many policies of which were subsequently incorporated into the Wagner Act in 1935), it marked the culmination of more than a quarter century of efforts to secure effective Federal legislation in the area of labor relations.

More important, it laid much of the groundwork for the Wagner Act and the Taft-Hartley Act, which provide the basic legal framework in which today's labor-management relations are conducted. The Railway Labor Act thus marks the transition in labor relations, not only from common law to statute law, but also from a public policy of opposition to one of acceptance of unionism and collective bargaining.

Although there is a popular tendency to identify this historic change in the national labor policy with Franklin Delano Roosevelt and the New Deal, it is an interesting footnote to political history that in fact the shift was initiated under Republican administrations. In 1926, when the Railway Labor Act was passed, Calvin Coolidge was President, while another Republican administration, that of Herbert Hoover, was the one during which the Norris-LaGuardia Act became law in 1932. Clearly, our present labor policy cannot be regarded simply as a Democratic legacy.

The Railway Labor Act of 1926 not only established that "Employees shall have the right to organize and bargain collectively through representatives of their own choosing," but also took steps to insure the effectiveness of this right in practice, by prohibiting employers from interfering in any way with the organization of its employees and by requiring them to bargain with the unions thus selected. Here, in brief, is the essence of present-day labor policy.

But the Act itself was only one side of the coin, for as we have seen, previous attempts at Federal legislation in industrial relations had been nullified by adverse court decisions. The other half of the coin, therefore, is the Texas and New Orleans case of 1930, in which the Supreme Court upheld the constitutionality of the Act and confirmed that the terms of the statute were in fact legitimate and proper expressions of public policy, although, of course, they applied only to railroads and not to interstate commerce generally.

Norris-LaGuardia Act

The Norris-LaGuardia Act, passed in 1932, is generally referred to as the anti-injunction act because of the elaborate restrictions it places upon the use of injunctions in labor disputes, with the objective of taking the disputes out of the hands of the Federal courts, for all practical purposes, and leaving them to be settled by the parties themselves. Norris-LaGuardia, in a sense, was the logical public policy sequel to the Railway Labor Act, for while the latter had established the principle that union activity should be free from *employer* interference, Norris-LaGuardia substantially freed union activity from *court* interference. Federal courts were forbidden to issue either temporary or permanent injunctions in labor disputes, except in "strict conformity" with the provisions of the Act. No peaceful or nonfraudulent union activity, including strikes and picketing, was subject to injunction. And in cases where the issuance of injunctions was not forbidden outright, the procedures and criteria for imposing an injunction were spelled out in detail in the law, rather than being left up to the judgment of the individual court.

In addition to thus defining and limiting the jurisdiction of the courts in labor disputes, the Act also made illegal the infamous "yellow-dog" contract —a contract, signed as a condition of employment, in which the employee agreed not to join a union on penalty of discharge—so called because only a "yellow dog" would take a job with such conditions imposed on him. But since employment pressures *did* force many workers to accept such terms, Norris-LaGuardia was a part of the trend to protect employees against such interference.

While the Norris-LaGuardia Act forbade yellow-dog contracts, it merely extended to interstate commerce in general a protection first provided employees in the Railway Labor Act in 1926. And the Railway Labor Act, in turn, is noteworthy in this respect because it was the first *Federal* statute to ban yellow-dog contracts, although some fifteen states had enacted such legislation as early as the 1890's.

NIRA

In 1933 came the first of the New Deal laws to deal with labor relations— the National Industrial Recovery Act, or NIRA. Legally speaking, the NIRA was schizophrenic, for it contained both the famous Section 7(a), which extended into interstate commerce generally the labor policies laid down in the Railway Labor Act, and provisions exempting from the antitrust laws business practices which complied with the NIRA codes for regulating prices and production.

Although the NIRA was declared unconstitutional in May 1935, after less than two years of existence, it nonetheless made a lasting contribution to public policy, since the interpretations and decisions of the numerous cases arising under Section 7(a) became the basis for the unfair labor practice provisions of the Wagner Act, enacted in June 1935, just one month after the decision ending the NIRA.[5]

[5] For an interesting discussion of Section 7 (a), see Millis and Montgomery, *op. cit.*, pp. 521–522.

Wagner Act

From organized labor's point of view, the high-water mark in Federal labor legislation was undoubtedly the National Labor Relations Act of 1935, commonly known as the Wagner Act.

Since its immediate predecessor, the NIRA, had been found unconstitutional by the Supreme Court, the status of the Wagner Act, which so closely resembled the labor sections of the NIRA, obviously needed to be settled in court. That test came in 1937, when the Supreme Court heard arguments in the famous Jones and Laughlin case. To the surprise of those who expected it to follow the lines of the NIRA decision, not only was the constitutionality of the Wagner Act upheld, but perhaps even more important in terms of its long-run impact, the court ruled that the provisions of the Wagner Act applied to manufacturing. Thus, by a broad interpretation of what affected commerce, it initiated an extension of the commerce power of Congress, which not only largely determined the impact of the Wagner Act, but laid the groundwork for a general extension of the regulatory powers of the Federal government as well.

It was only after this decision that the full impact of the Wagner Act was felt. Between 1937 and 1947, the year the Wagner Act was amended by the passage of the Taft-Hartley Act, a major change in the industrial-relations climate of the United States took place, in large part because of the impact of the Wagner Act. The objective of the law was simple enough—to protect the right of the American worker to join unions if he so desired, free from interference by the employer. It is no secret that the Wagner Act was "pro-labor"—openly and avowedly meant to support and encourage union activity and collective bargaining. Its preamble, in fact, declares United States policy to be that of "encouraging the practice and procedure of collective bargaining" and of "protecting the exercise by workers of full freedom of association, self-organization, and designation of representatives of their own choosing, for the purpose of negotiating the terms and conditions of their employment or other mutual aid or protection."[6] A more concise and open statement of the Congressional intention to support and encourage union activity and collective bargaining would be hard to find.

Let us briefly examine the reasons for the adoption of such a policy. *Why* should Congress be so concerned with promoting collective bargaining? Why should it be necessary to protect the right of workers to join unions?

To correct a widespread misunderstanding of the Wagner Act, we hasten to add that it did not legalize either the existence of unions or the process of bargaining; the right of workers to join unions and to bargain collectively had been established long before the Wagner Act and, in fact, had not been

[6] The Wagner Act, Section 1, "Findings and Policy," as quoted in Witney, *op. cit.*, p. 677.

seriously challenged since the demise of the conspiracy doctrine. The Wagner Act was designed to *protect* those rights and make them effective in practice as well as in theory.

The problem to which the Wagner Act addressed itself was the interference with those previously recognized rights. For the fact is that the *right* to join a union was of little or no practical value to a worker so long as his employer was free to fire him if he exercised it. And indeed, until the passage of the Wagner Act, this was the fundamental weakness in the civil rights of the industrial worker; economically, the right to join a union was often practically meaningless. Accordingly, the Wagner Act was designed to protect the worker's civil rights by making it illegal for employers to interfere in his exercise of them. And indeed, the logic of this is evident (whether you agree with it or not): why should the exercise of a legal *right* (the right to join a union) be grounds for discharge or discrimination? This was one basis for the Wagner Act, which was in fact a civil-rights law, in the current sense of that phrase.

The Wagner Act was also a recognition of a long-standing economic concept—that the individual worker was unable to bargain on equal terms with the modern business organization and that, unless he was free to organize and join unions to restore the balance, economic circumstances and the imperfections of the labor market would often force him to accept jobs with undesirably low wages and poor working conditions. Stripped of its elaborate rhetoric, the Wagner Act recognized that competition between workers for jobs tended, like competition in other markets, to force down the price of labor; but unlike competition in other markets, lowering the price of labor involved a social cost, presumably one outweighing the social benefit. Accordingly, by protecting the right to organize and to join unions, competition in the labor market would be reduced and the standards of living of the working man protected.

Finally, the Wagner Act was implicit recognition of the fact that in a country which grants universal manhood suffrage and in which all adults have the right to vote and to participate in their government, it is only consistent to provide for democracy in the plant through the mechanism of the labor organization.

Surprisingly enough, only three basic techniques for achieving its objectives were provided in the original Wagner Act. First, the Act prohibited employer conduct designed to interfere with the worker's right to join a union. The nature of this conduct was spelled out in detail in five types of so-called "unfair labor practices" (an inept and confusing term for unfair *employer* practices with respect to labor), which we will describe later in the chapter.

Second, the Act afforded industrial workers and unions a new method of organizing—the secret-ballot election. By means of a secret-ballot election, workers could now *vote* to be represented by a union. And simple and logical as this technique may seem, it represented a major social innovation, providing a peaceful and orderly way of unionizing, a substitute for organizing by resort to economic pressure.

Finally, the Act established a quasi-judicial agency, the National Labor Relations Board (NLRB), whose function and duty was to enforce and administer the law, to listen to charges of unfair labor practices and to decide on them, and to administer the secret-ballot elections.

Basically, that was all there was to the law. Yet in the ten years between the Jones and Laughlin decision and the enactment of the Taft-Hartley amendments to the Wagner Act, these three provisions virtually revolutionized the conduct of American industrial relations and were a major factor in the vast expansion of union membership from 3 million in 1935 to 14 million in 1947. How much of this expansion was due to the Wagner Act, of course, we cannot tell, but it seems inescapable that it was instrumental, and fundamentally so, in bringing about the great change.

Operation of the Act

These three basic provisions have fundamentally changed the theory and practice of industrial relations in the United States. A brief explanation of how they operate follows.[7]

Unfair labor practices   The Wagner Act prohibits employers from engaging in five *types* of practice considered to interfere with the workers rights regarding unions. Since the types of prohibited conduct are defined in rather broad terms, it is up to the National Labor Relations Board in each case to decide whether the particular conduct with which an employer is charged comes under the law (and, of course, whether the alleged conduct in fact occurred). Employers are forbidden to:

1. *Interfere, restrain, or coerce employees in their union activities.* Threatening employees with loss of their jobs or loss of benefits if they join a union, threatening to close the plant and, if a union is organized in it, granting wage increases deliberately timed to prevent unionization are examples of behavior prohibited by the law.

2. *Assist or dominate a labor organization.* "Puppet" unions controlled or supported by the employer are prohibited.

3. *Discriminate in employment for union membership or union activities, or lack of them.* This forbids, for example, demoting or discharging an

---

[7] This section is based on material in *Federal Labor Laws and Programs,* Bulletin No. 262 (Washington, D.C.: U.S. Department of Labor, Bureau of Labor Standards, 1964), pp. 14–17.

employee because he urged his fellow employees to join a union and refusal to hire a qualified applicant for a job because he belongs to a union.

4. *Discriminate for participation in NLRB proceedings.* This is designed to prevent discrimination against employees who bring charges against their employer under this law.

5. *Refuse to bargain collectively with a certified union.* Refusing to put into written form agreements reached with a certified union, giving a wage increase larger than that offered to the union, and refusing to deal with union representatives because the employees are out on strike violate this section of the law.

In unfair-practice cases, where the Board finds the employer (or now, the union) guilty of a violation of the law, any one of several different actions may result, depending upon the nature of the violation. If it finds that an employee was discharged because of union membership or union activity (the most frequent unfair-practice charge), the Board may order his reinstatement, with or without back pay. If it finds that employer conduct interfered with the workers' decision to vote for or against a union, the Board may call for a new election. In other cases, the conduct in question may simply be ordered stopped.

Secret-ballot elections   In order for the NLRB to conduct one of the secret-ballot elections (called "a representation election") by which workers choose whether they wish to be represented by a union, the union (the customary petitioner for an election) must first demonstrate that there is a bona fide interest among workers in being represented. By a rule-of-thumb process, it was early decided that if 30 per cent of the workers in a bargaining unit were interested in having an election and demonstrated this interest by submitting authorization cards, petitions, or other means, an election would be held. Similarly, if an employer calls for an election, the Board must hold a hearing to determine whether it is justified. Before the election is held, the Board must decide, in conjunction with the employer and the union, which employees are eligible to vote. The question as to which workers are eligible to vote comes under the rather misleading heading of "appropriate bargaining unit"—a term which, in the secret-ballot election process, really involves the question of the appropriate *voting* unit; it is only after the election is over and the union has won that it becomes in fact an appropriate *bargaining* unit.

The boundaries of the bargaining unit, or voting unit, may vary widely. It may be limited to a particular group of employees in a particular plant, such as skilled craftsmen, or it may consist of all production workers in the plant; it may include workers in more than one plant of the same employer, or it may be so broad as to include workers in plants of several employers—a so-called multiemployer unit.

In any case, the question of the appropriate bargaining unit may prove a difficult one. If the employer and the union agree as to the appropriate unit, well and good; the Board will probably determine that to be the appropriate unit. But if the employer and union disagree or if competing unions disagree, as they often do, the decision in practice then falls on the Board—and its decision as to the appropriate voting unit may well be, under certain circumstances, the key factor in the final outcome of the election.

So far as the election itself is concerned, the outcome is decided by a simple majority of those votes *cast,* rather than a majority of eligible votes; regardless of the number of employees *eligible* to vote, therefore, any number greater than 50 per cent of the votes *cast* will be decisive. Although, conceivably, the actions of a small fraction of eligible employees could determine the outcome of an election binding on many workers, in practice nearly 90 per cent of those eligible to vote do so; the number who passively acquiesce by "letting George do it" is normally, therefore, quite small. And if a majority of those voting cast their vote for a union, the union is then certified by the Board as the authorized bargaining representative for *all* employees in the bargaining unit. It then becomes the legal duty of the employer to bargain with it; to fail to do so is an unfair labor practice.

But here a caution is in order—the requirement to *bargain* is *not* a requirement to *agree* to the unions demands, either in full or in part. It is simply a duty to negotiate with the union. This point, however, is the source of much confusion at present, for it now involves the question of whether an employer is bargaining in good faith—whether he is genuinely complying or is, in fact, complying only nominally. And without question, the most interesting recent case involving this question is the long-fought case between General Electric Company and the National Labor Relations Board.

The National Labor Relations Board   As created by the terms of the Wagner Act, the NLRB is an independent agency of the Federal government. It has, however, no independent power to enforce its decisions, and if an employer or union fails to comply with its orders, the Board must ask a U.S. Court of Appeals for an enforcement decree. If a court decree is issued, failure to comply becomes contempt of court and is punishable accordingly. At the same time, Board decisions are themselves subject to appeal up to and including the Supreme Court.

Although the enforcement of the Wagner Act (as amended by Taft-Hartley and Landrum-Griffin) is one of its primary functions, the Board can deal only with cases submitted to it; charges of unfair labor practices or requests for representation elections must be made to the Board before it can enter a case. Because it is a quasi-judicial agency, the Board's decisions as to whether particular conduct violates the law serve to put flesh on the bare bones of the statute; just as the decisions of the court provide the common law, so the decisions of the NLRB have the force and effect of law. The Board's interpretation of the statute from case to case and from day to day determines the details of public policy; its interpretations are the law of the land so far as labor relations are concerned.

In this situation, it is hardly surprising that the Board's interpretations of the legality of employer and union conduct have often been the center of controversy, or that the Board should be the subject of argument and debate aimed at modifying its decisions in favor of one interest group or the other. Thus, almost since its creation in 1935, the Board has been accused by employers and employer organizations of being pro-labor, of partisan interpretation of the law in favor of unions.

Less widely realized, perhaps, is that the Board has been almost as vehemently criticized by organized labor. In 1955, for instance, when a majority of the five-man Board were Eisenhower appointees, the American Federation of Labor complained that "The record of the Board's decisions in the past year has been one of repeated hostility to unions and partiality to employers. Administering an anti-union law, the Board has taken advantage of almost every opportunity to tip the scales even further against unions."[8]

And since Board members are Presidential appointees, it is not surprising that the appointments should reflect the political leanings and spirit of the administration in office. But quite aside from the evaluation of the tenor of the Board's decisions over the past thirty years, it should be remembered that the Wagner Act and, no less certainly, the Taft-Hartley Act establish the over-all framework within which the Board's decisions and judgments must be made. Taft-Hartley has not significantly changed the basic intent of the Wagner Act, which is to encourage collective bargaining as a process, and unions as institutions. This objective is the statutory mandate within which the Board must operate; it cannot legally do otherwise.

Any fair evaluation of the Board's decisions, therefore, must take this fact into account. The Board can hardly be accused of partisan behavior if the regulations which it is called upon to interpret are essentially pro-labor in the first place. The criteria by which the Board's role would have to be judged are (1) whether its interpretations effectively depart from the intent of Congress when it drafted the law, and (2) whether, within the area of its discretion, it consistently or persistently tips the scales in favor (say) of labor. And, of course, in interpreting a law sections of which were enacted twenty or thirty years ago, the Board increasingly encounters situations which were not taken into consideration when the law was written; in these cases, it may very well have to venture into new policy determinations for which the

[8] *Proceedings,* Seventy-fourth Convention of the American Federation of Labor, New York City, 1955, p. 191.

statute itself gives little if any guidance. And finally, it should be noted that in so controversial an area as labor relations policy, where there are no scientific answers and no pat formulas, the question of what is "sound" or "good" public policy is often, in the last analysis, a question of the values one holds.

Without trying to appraise the content of the Board's decisions, one measure of the Board's performance over the years may be found in the record of cases appealed to the courts for review and enforcement by the Board or by employers and unions contesting the Board's decisions.

Of the 2,931 cases decided by Courts of Appeals in the thirty years from July 5, 1935, to June 30, 1965, the courts affirmed Board orders in full in 57.4 per cent of the cases and with modifications in 20.2 per cent. Board orders were set aside only 17.5 per cent of the time.

And of the 159 cases that reached the Supreme Court between 1935 and 1965, the Board's decisions were affirmed in full 61.7 per cent of the time and with modification 8.2 per cent of the time, and were set aside in only 17.6 per cent of the cases. Over all, then, the Board's decisions and interpretations have been upheld in the courts more than three times as often as they have been overruled.[9]

Taft-Hartley Act

The state of the unions in 1947 was remarkably different from what it had been in 1935, the year the Wagner Act was passed. Under the combined stimulus of the Wagner Act and the economic expansion of World War II, union membership had risen more than 10 million, from around 3.6 million to 13.9 million; unions had penetrated the mass-production industries, and individual unions had grown to unprecedented sizes. Unions had been touched by success beyond their wildest dreams.

This very success, however, stirred a vital nerve in the American character —fear of bigness *per se*. The feeling that labor had become too big and too powerful, and that such power had to be checked and brought under control, gained increasing momentum (no doubt prompted by employers anxious to keep unions from threatening *their* power).

When, on the termination of wartime controls, pent-up energy was released in the form of a wave of strikes, it was the signal for the passage of the Taft-Hartley Act, alternatively described by its advocates as a way of restoring the balance of power between labor and management and by its critics as a "slave-labor" law.

It should be realized from the outset that the Wagner Act was not repealed by the passage of the Taft-Hartley Act; Taft-Hartley is an *amendment* to the

[9] *Thirtieth Annual Report of the National Labor Relations Board,* 1965, p. 212.

Wagner Act, not a replacement or a substitute for it. And the provisions of the Wagner Act, therefore, are still in full force and effect, although they have been supplemented by the provisions of Taft-Hartley.

Quite aside from the specific and detailed differences in the provisions of the Wagner Act and the Taft-Hartley Act is the fundamental difference in their philosophy and in their relationship to what is presently described as free collective bargaining. The role of government vis-à-vis the collective-bargaining process is significantly different in the two laws.

The difference is this: the Wagner Act was designed to encourage collective bargaining and, under specified circumstances, to require it. Once a union had been certified as the representative of the workers in an appropriate bargaining unit, the employer no longer had the option to bargain or not as he saw fit; he was required to bargain, but he was not required to submit to union demands. Furthermore, the terms of the agreement were not regulated; whatever agreement was reached between a union and a company was acceptable under the Wagner Act. Thus, in effect, the role of the government, under Wagner, was to get the parties to the bargaining table and to get the bargaining process under way, and no more. The content of the agreement was not at issue.

With Taft-Hartley, this situation changed. The old requirements to bargain were retained, but now the content of the agreement was subject to regulation; even if both parties wanted it, for example, a closed-shop provision could not be included in a union contract with an employer engaged in interstate commerce. The area of government regulation, in short, was extended from the *process* of collective bargaining to the *terms* of the collective-bargaining agreement; it was a step looked on with concern by the devotees of free (unregulated) collective bargaining on both sides of the table.

The stated purpose of the Taft-Hartley Act is brief and to the point, namely, "to provide additional facilities for mediation of labor disputes affecting commerce, to equalize legal responsibilities of labor organizations and employers, and for other purposes."

Unfair Union Practices

As a means of equalizing the responsibilities of unions and employers, Congress balanced the unfair labor-practice provisions of the Wagner Act (which, as we have seen, regulated *employer* conduct in labor relations) with a set of six categories of unfair *union* practices.[10] Under Section 8(b) of the law, unions may not:

1. *Restrain or coerce employees* in the exercise of their right to join

---

[10] *Federal Labor Laws and Programs*, Bulletin No. 262, *op. cit.*, pp. 17–20.

unions of their own choosing or to refrain from joining a union. This basically parallels the prohibition on employers.

2. *Cause discrimination for union activities.* This prohibits unions from trying to cause employers to engage in the unfair labor practice of discrimination for union activity.

3. *Refuse to bargain with an employer* when the union is the certified representative of the workers. This parallels the prohibition on employers.

4. *Engage in secondary boycotts.* Probably the most complex provision in Taft-Hartley, this section is intended to define and regulate the use of an economic weapon of unions and to minimize the use of innocent third parties as tools in disputes between unions and employers.

5. *Charge excessive or discriminatory initiation fees.* What constitutes an excessive or discriminatory fee is left to the judgment of the NLRB.

6. *Featherbed.* Although defined here as causing an employer to pay for services not performed, generally speaking, the problem of featherbedding is not concerned with whether services are performed for pay, but with whether or not they are *necessary.*

In addition to defining these unfair *union* practices, Taft-Hartley contained a complex variety of amendments of the Wagner Act such as those detailing regulation of union security practices; providing new regulations with regard to employee elections; providing for damage suits against unions; requiring financial and constitutional reports from unions and non-Communist affidavits from their officers; authorizing and, in some cases, requiring the NLRB to use injunctions to prevent unfair labor practices; and establishing the injunction as a means of coping with national emergency strikes. (Some of these provisions, in turn, have since been amended by Title VII of the Landrum-Griffin Act, which contains amendments to Taft-Hartley and is separate and distinct from the main body of the Landrum-Griffin Act.)

Union Security

As it now stands, the *closed shop,* which requires employees to be union members *before* they are hired, is illegal in interstate commerce generally, except in the building and construction industry where the prohibition proved unenforceable because the closed shop met the needs of both employers and unions.

The *union shop,* in which the employee must join the union *after* being hired, may now be negotiated without special formality, except in "right-to-work" states, where state law prohibits both union shop and closed shop.

In addition, even though a union shop or closed shop exists, neither employees who have been refused union membership nor members who have lost their membership are to be discriminated against—i.e., fired—unless they were refused membership or lost their membership status for refusal to pay dues and/or initiation fees.

Because the "right-to-work" laws are the outgrowth of Section 14(b) of Taft-Hartley (a unique clause that, in cases where they conflict, permits state law to supersede Federal law as to the union shop), the fight over the right-to-work issue was focused in 1965 and 1966 on that section. Had it been repealed, as labor urged, the customary priority of Federal over state law would have been restored and state right-to-work laws automatically rendered invalid.

Elections

To the representation elections provided for in the Wagner Act, Taft-Hartley adds two other types of elections—the decertification election, in which employees vote whether they want to stop being represented by their union, and the deauthorization election, in which they vote whether to continue the right of their union to make a union-shop contract.

Although decertification is doubtless a desirable safeguard for employees dissatisfied with the efficacy of their union, in practical terms it is relatively unimportant. In 1965, for example, out of a total of 7,824 elections conducted under the law, only 200, or less than 3 per cent of all elections, involved decertification. Of these 200 cases, unions lost in 128, involving 4,718 employees, and won in 72, involving 7,847 employees.

The same conclusion holds for the deauthorization election, of which there were only 48 in 1965, involving a total of 3,976 employees. Unions' right to make union-shop agreements was withdrawn in 35 cases, representing 2,759 employees, or an average of 79 employees per election.[11]

Labor Disputes

To facilitate the achievement of collective-bargaining agreements and to help settle disputes, Taft-Hartley created the Federal Mediation and Conciliation Service (FMCS) as an independent agency and required that, thirty days before the expiration date of any existing contract, the parties to it must notify the FMCS that a labor dispute exists (unless of course they have already reached agreement on a new contract). The point, of course, is to make mediation and conciliation available before a crisis is reached (although the parties are under no obligation to accept FMCS aid).

More dramatic, though probably no more important in the long-run, are the provisions for handling so-called "national-emergency strikes"—strikes which may "imperil the national health or safety." Under this provision,

[11] *Ibid.,* pp. 16–20.

when the President of the United States thinks a national emergency exists or is pending as a result of a strike, he appoints a board to determine the issues in the dispute. After the board reports to him, he directs the Attorney General to seek an eighty-day injunction from a United States district court, which requires employees to return (or continue) to work for that period. After sixty days, if the dispute has not been settled, the board of inquiry reports on the state of the dispute and makes public the employer's "last offer." The employees, in secret ballot, vote whether to accept the "last offer." If a settlement has not been reached at the end of eighty days, the injunction expires and the parties are free to return to their strike or lockout, in which case the President is left to recommend further action to Congress.

From 1947 through 1966 the Taft-Hartley injunction was used 25 times—an average of a little more than once a year. But the number of industries in which it has been used is small; until November 1966, only ten were involved, with most of the injunctions concentrated in five of the ten industries—longshoring (6), atomic energy (4), and coal, maritime, and aerospace (3 each). The other industries involved were steel (2), and, once each, meat-packing, telephones, copper, and electrical manufacturing.[12]

From this brief glimpse at the record, it is evident that whether a strike or threatened strike is likely to be classed a national emergency is to a large extent dependent upon the nature of the industry and upon whether its service or product is really a necessity for which there is no effective substitute and whose use we cannot reasonably delay.

A more important issue, of course, is how effective the Taft-Hartley injunction has been in settling the disputes in which it has been employed. In at least seven cases, strikes occurred or were resumed after the eighty-day injunction had expired.[13] Furthermore, it seems evident, on the basis of both logic and experience, that the requirement of a secret-ballot vote by employees on whether to accept or reject the employer's last offer is a waste of time and an indication of the Congress' basic misunderstanding of collective-bargaining tactics.

If, as the Congressional draftsmen of this provision obviously expected, a secret ballot would give the members the chance to express their true feelings and thus prevent "dictatorial" labor leaders from keeping them out on strike against their wishes, one would expect to find a number of instances where this expectation was realized. In actual practice, however, in *none* of the 14 cases where a vote was actually held on the employer's last offer did the membership vote to accept! The reason, on reflection, seems clear—

---

[12] *National Emergency Disputes Under the Labor Management Relations (Taft-Hartley) Act, 1947–1965,* U.S. Department of Labor, Bureau of Labor Statistics, Bulletin No. 1482 (Washington, D.C.: U.S. Government Printing Office, 1966), p. 1. The twenty-fifth injunction was issued in October 1966, in the dispute between the General Electric Company and a coalition of unions.
[13] *Ibid.,* p. 2.

regardless of whether the members *wanted* the strike (a meaningless term in such a situation), by *rejecting* the employer's last offer the workers expect to force him to raise it. And, indeed, in at least five of the cases where the last offer was rejected by membership vote, the final settlement *was* higher than the "last offer."

It should be pointed out, of course, that the fact that the President has the *authority* to initiate this procedure is no guarantee that he will use it. In 1952, in order to avert a threatened steel strike, President Truman seized the steel industry rather than invoke the Taft-Hartley Act. And more recently, President Johnson was criticized in some quarters for failure to utilize the Taft-Hartley injunction in connection with the New York City transit strike of January 1966.

Landrum-Griffin Act

We have noted before that a vital union function is to bring a greater degree of democracy into business organizations by providing employees with a mechanism by which they can participate in the decisions regarding their terms of employment. Paradoxically, as unions grew in size and influence, the question was raised with increasing frequency whether positive steps, in the form of legislation, were needed to protect the rights of the union member (and the would-be member) and to insure that he had as great a voice in the decisions of his union as his union gave him in the decisions of his employer.

One of the first to focus on the question of internal union democracy was the American Civil Liberties Union, whose study, "Democracy in Trade Unions," recommending a bill of rights for union members, was published in 1943.[14] During the 1950's there were a number of governmental investigations into various aspects of union administration, ranging from the 1952–1953 hearings of the New York State Crime Commission on racketeering on the New York City waterfront (involving the International Longshoremen's Association) to investigations of the mismanagement of union pension funds, which led to the passage of the Welfare and Pension Plans Disclosure Act of 1958.

The last and, by long odds, the most widely publicized of these was the Congressional investigation held by the McClellan Committee, or more accurately, the Select Committee on Improper Activities in the Labor or Management Field. From 1957 through 1959 the McClellan Committee held 270 days of hearings, heard 1,526 witnesses, and produced 58 volumes of testi-

[14] Joel Seidman, "Emergence of Concern with Union Government and Administration," in Marten S. Estey, Philip Taft, and Martin Wagner, eds., *Regulating Union Government* (New York: Harper & Row, 1964), p. 4.

mony, over half of which were devoted to evidence of various types of racketeering and corruption in the Teamsters Union. The bulk of the Committee's attention, in fact, was focused on just 7 unions out of the more than 180 international unions then active. The risks of generalizing from these limited findings are obvious.[15]

The results of the McClellan Committee hearings were substantial and varied. They made Jimmy Hoffa, president of the Teamsters, a national figure (albeit a controversial one) and contributed not a little to the public awareness of the then Senator John F. Kennedy and his brother, Robert. They led the AFL-CIO to adopt a six-part code of ethical practices and to expel three unions—the Teamsters, the Laundry Workers, and the Bakery and Confectionery Workers—whose leaders were accused of violating these codes. From a public policy standpoint, however, most significant was the impetus they gave for the passage of legislation to correct these abuses—the Labor-Management Reporting and Disclosure Act of 1959, commonly referred to as the Landrum-Griffin Act.

The Landrum-Griffin Act consists of seven sections, or titles; the first six regulate internal union practices, and the seventh contains amendments to the Taft-Hartley Act (as described previously). The first five, which include the basic elements of the law of internal union government, are summarized briefly here.[16]

Bill of Rights

The law begins with a bill of rights for union members, designed to insure certain standards of democracy within unions and to guarantee the individual due process in his role as a union member. Specifically, the law provides members:

1. Equal right to attend, participate in, and vote at meetings and elections, subject to reasonable union rules.

2. Freedom to meet and assemble with other members, to express any arguments or opinions, and to voice views upon candidates and business properly before a meeting.

3. Protection from increases in dues or the imposition of assessments, except where specified procedures are followed, including secret ballot, referendum, or national union convention.

4. Protection of the right to testify, communicate with legislators, and bring suit for relief (from infringement of rights by the union) after using remedies available to them within the union.

5. The right to copies of bargaining agreements.

6. The right to be informed by the union of their rights under this law.

[15] *Ibid.,* p. 6–7.
[16] *Federal Labor Laws and Programs,* Bulletin No. 262, *op. cit.,* pp. 40–52.

7. The right to notice and fair hearing before any disciplinary actions are taken against them by the union, except for nonpayment of dues.

When these rights are infringed upon, they are enforced, not by turning to an administrative agency (as in the case of the Wagner and Taft-Hartley Acts), but by filing suit in Federal District courts, a procedure which may well tend to reduce the ability of the average union member to use the law for his own protection.

Reporting

Following the bill of rights is the reporting provision, which requires each labor organization to file with the Secretary of Labor annual financial reports covering its assets and liabilities; a detailed income and expenditures statement, including, among other items, the payments to all union officers, loans to union officers, and loans to businesses; and copies of their constitution and by-laws, with annual reports of any changes made in them. In addition, union officers and employees must report "conflict of interest" financial transactions with businesses the union may deal with; similar reports are required from employers and labor consultants.

The reporting requirement itself is not new; indeed, the Taft-Hartley Act contained a compulsory reporting provision twelve years before the passage of the Landrum-Griffin Act. What is new is that these mandatory union reports became subject to public disclosure. Copies of all reports required by the law are available for inspection or purchase in Labor Department Offices; anyone may see them, for any reason.

Public disclosure of financial and administrative details of union government was designed as one of the methods by which the Landrum-Griffin Act would stimulate higher standards of union conduct. As the Bureau of Labor-Management Reports noted in 1960: "The law relies heavily upon the principles of reporting and disclosure to eliminate abuses in the labor-management field. It assumes that democracy in the labor movement is strengthened when union members have detailed essential information about their union and how its affairs are being handled."[17]

Trusteeship

The use of trusteeships—in which national unions take control, for one reason or another, of a local union—is also regulated; the local union is thus protected by the law, just as the individual member is. Basically, the purposes for which trusteeships are permitted are limited, and the national union is required, where a trusteeship continues more than six months, to show why it has not been terminated.

[17] *Report of the Bureau of Labor-Management Reports,* 1960, *op. cit.,* p. 16.

This provision was included in the Landrum-Griffin Act because the Mc-Clellan Committee hearings indicated that trusteeships were sometimes used to "milk" local union treasuries or to control local union votes so as to help perpetuate national union officers in power. On the other hand, it was equally clear that trusteeships had a proper function as well and that they were often used to provide assistance to locals in difficulty and to protect the membership from improper conduct of *local* union officers. The problem of devising an effective regulation, therefore, was to distinguish between "proper" and "improper" trusteeships—between "good" and "bad" ones.

In his 1962 report to Congress on the operation of trusteeship provisions, the Secretary of Labor found 777 trusteeships in effect, covering only 1 per cent of all local unions.[18]

Elections

Since elections provide the principal mechanism by which the membership can exercise its role in the government of unions, Congress took steps in the law to insure both reasonable frequency and regularity of elections and proper election procedures. Accordingly, the law established maximum intervals between union elections of five years for national or international unions, four for intermediate bodies, and three for local unions, and specified standards for the conduct of elections, such as the requirement of secret ballots, provision for a fair chance for the "opposition," and protection of the members' right to vote.

Fiduciary Responsibilities

The Landrum-Griffin Act holds that union officers and representatives occupy positions of trust and must, therefore, administer the organization solely for the benefit of its members and in accordance with its own constitutions and by-laws. The act requires officers to be bonded, restricts the uses of union funds, and restricts employer payments and loans to union officials. More important, union officers who are alleged to have violated their trust may be sued, not only by the union, but by the individual union member as well.

Evaluation of Landrum-Griffin Act

The passage of the Landrum-Griffin Act and the experience with its provisions in the seven years since its passage suggest that the key issue lies not

[18] *Union Trusteeships* (Washington, D.C.: U.S. Department of Labor, Bureau of Labor-Management Reports, 1962), p. 6.

in any single provision of the law but in whether it has achieved a better balance than existed before between the rights of individual members on the one hand and the needs of the organization for stability and efficiency on the other. It has become increasingly evident, for example, that greater democracy and a greater rank-and-file voice in union affairs, especially in bargaining and negotiating, is as likely to mean a more militant posture as it is a more flexible one. In many cases, union leaders have found themselves unable to secure ratification of agreements reached with management, and have been forced to return to the bargaining table in search of further concessions. By 1965, in fact, industrial-relations directors in major industries were publicly admitting their concern over this turn of events and referring wistfully to the days of "responsible" union leadership when a union negotiator could settle on the spot, sure in the knowledge that his membership would accept his recommendations.

Whether this tendency on the whole has become a threat to the effectiveness of collective bargaining and whether it has led to unreasonably expensive economic settlements is not known, and perhaps can never be known. But the issue is no less real because of this; such costs as these must constantly and continually be weighed, however subjectively and inaccurately, against the benefits of greater membership participation in business decision-making.

Epilogue

The Future of Unionism

The past 80 years have seen the development of two notably successful models of labor organization—the craft-union model and the industrial-union model. Today, the great question is whether there is a union model which will not only meet the needs of white-collar workers, but will also attract them as members.

In some respects the situation confronting the labor movement today resembles that which existed in 1935. Like the mass-production workers in 1935, the white-collar workers today are a vast and largely unclaimed territory for organized labor. And as unions in 1935 had to organize the mass-production workers if they were to regain or increase their relative status in the labor force, so unions today must organize the white-collar workers if they are to regain the relative position they had a decade ago.

In some ways, however, the problem is more difficult than that which faced the leaders of the American Federation of Labor thirty-odd years ago. For then, as we have seen, while there was violent disagreement within the labor movement on the question of industrial organization, the question that divided the AFL and led to the formation of the CIO was not whether industrial unionism *could* reach the mass production workers, but whether it *should,* and in so doing interfere with the potential rights of the craft unions.

This time, almost regrettably, there is no such conflict. There is no group which knows, or even claims that it knows, the obvious formula for organizing white-collar workers. *This* time there is no question that the white-collar worker *should* be organized, but whether he *can* be organized on a substantial scale, and if so, how.

And there is still one further problem. There is an uneasy feeling in some union circles that perhaps the organizational model for white-collar workers, like the organizational model for professional and scientific workers, may not be a *union* model at all, but one that more closely resembles a professional association, like the National Education Association, the American Association of University Professors, or the Nurses Association.

The recent activities of some of the professional groups—nurses, teachers, even physicians—suggest that they may adopt union tactics and union strategies without becoming unions.

If there is a competition between organizational models to win the membership of the growing white-collar group, which model will win—the union model or the professional association model, or some hybrid version of the two?[1]

---

[1] For an interesting analysis along these lines, see George Strauss, "Professionalism and Occupational Associations," *Industrial Relations,* May 1963, pp. 7–31.

Index

Page numbers followed by *n* indicate references to footnotes.

Abel, I. W., 60
AFL, 14, 15, 16, 26, 27, 106, 117
  and craft unionism, 16–21
  and exclusive jurisdiction, policy of, 17, 18, 21, 28
  membership of, 21, 25
  merger with CIO, 17, 21, 29–32
  and politics, 20
  structure and policies of, 16, 17–21
  and trade autonomy, policy of, 17–18, 29
AFL-CIO, 10, 21, 29, 39, 43, 53
  Building and Construction Trades Department of, 44
  codes of ethical practices adopted by, 32, 113
  and COPE, 29
  Executive Council of, 54
  functions of, 36–37
  membership of, 29, 30, 33, 36
  structure of, 35
  Teamsters Union expelled from, 32–33, 41, 113

Agricultural Workers Organizing Committee (AFL-CIO), 10
Alaska, number of union members in, 10
Amalgamated Clothing Workers, 7, 9
American Civil Liberties Union, 112
American Economic Association, 2
American Federation of Labor; *see* AFL
American Federation of Labor and Congress of Industrial Organizations; *see* AFL-CIO
American Motors Corporation, 60, 64
Antitrust laws, 26, 97, 98
Apathy, in union membership, 49, 51
Apex case, 98
Appropriate bargaining unit, determination of, 104–105
Auto Workers, United, 3, 7, 8, 23, 24, 25, 28, 32, 37, 40, 41, 59, 60, 64, 84, 91

Bakery and Confectionery Workers Union, 113
Barnett, George E., 2
Bates, Harry C., 54
Beck, Dave, 45
Bill of rights, in Landrum-Griffin Act, 113–14
Blue-collar workers, as base of labor movement, 4
Boycott, 75, 97
    injunction against, 95, 96
    secondary, prohibited by Taft-Hartley Act, 109
    and Sherman Antitrust Act, 97
Bricklayers Union, 40, 44, 54
Bridges, Harry, 28
Building Service Employees Union, 7
Building trades, collective-bargaining decisions in, 62–63
Building Trades Council, 44
Bureau of Labor Statistics, 7, 33, 37, 42, 52
Business cycle, and union growth, 83–87
Business unions, 21, 54, 68, 72–73

California:
    number of union members in, 9, 10
    right-to-work proposal defeated in, 68
Canada, 2, 37, 44
Carpenters Union, 7, 18, 21, 22, 26, 33, 37, 40, 44, 76
Chamberlain, Neil W., 19
Chrysler Motors Corporation, 60, 64
Cigar Makers Union, 16
CIO, 8, 14, 17, 29, 117
    formation of, 22–23, 28
    and industrial unions, 21–28
    membership of, 25
    merger with AFL, 17, 21, 29–32
    PAC established by, 29
City federations, 43
Civil Rights Act (1964), 9, 68, 70
Civil War, 13, 14
Clayton Act, 97, 98

Closed shop, 68, 79, 109
Clothing Workers, Amalgamated, 7, 9
Collective bargaining, 19, 36, 38, 73–75
    and agreements rejected by union membership, 48, 50, 58, 116
    decision-making in; see Decision-making, union
    and Taft-Hartley Act, 108, 110
    and Wagner Act, 108
Colorado, right-to-work proposal defeated in, 68
Committee on Political Education, 29
Common law, in labor relations, 93, 94, 98
Commonwealth v. Hunt, 94
Communications Association, American, 28
Communications Workers, 7
Communist-dominated unions, 86–87
    expelled from CIO, 27–28, 30, 41, 87
Congress of Industrial Organizations; see CIO
Conspicuous consumption, by labor leaders, 78
Conspiracy doctrine, of union activity, 94–95
COPE, 29
Cordwainers case, Philadelphia (1806), 65, 93, 94–95
Craft unions:
    advantage of, in collective-bargaining decisions, 60
    and AFL, 16–21
    beginnings of, 14
    defined, 14n
    jurisdictions of, 40
    and Knights of Labor, 15

Danbury Hatters case, 97, 98
Decision-making, union, in collective bargaining, 55–65, 74
    centralization of, 61–65
    and comparisons by rank-and-file, 56–57, 58
    economic factors in, 57

membership pressure in, 57–59
and reconciliation of conflicts within membership, 59–61
Depression, economic, and union growth, 83–84, 85, 86
DiGiorgio Corporation, 10
DuBay, Father, 11
Dubinsky, David, 55
Duplex Printing case, 97, 98

Elections, union, 29, 102–103, 104–105, 110, 115
of officers, 46, 47, 49–50
Electrical Workers unions, 7, 9, 10, 28, 44, 49, 55
Erdman Act, 99

Farm Workers Association, National, 10, 11
Farm Workers Organizing Committee, United (AFL-CIO), 10
Featherbedding, 109
Federal Mediation and Conciliation Service, 48, 110
Fees and dues, union, 70–71
Finances, union, 77–79
Ford, Henry, 25
Ford Motor Company, 27, 60, 64
Frontier unions, 10–11

Galenson, Walter, 23, 27
General Electric Company, 44, 105, 111*n*
General Motors Corporation, 23, 24, 52, 60, 64, 77, 84
General Motors Council, National (UAW), 64
Goldberg, Arthur J., 31
Gompers, Samuel, 16, 17, 18, 20, 21, 38, 72, 97
Goods-producing industries, and shift to service industries, 4
Gould, Jay, 15
Green, William, 31
Grievance procedure, 42, 73–74
Guidelines, wage, 91, 92

Hayes, A. J., 55
Haymarket riot (1886), 15–16
Hazard, Leland, 84–85
Healy, James J., 69
Hoffa, Jimmy, 32, 33, 39, 41, 43, 45, 54, 78, 91, 113
salary of, 52
Hoffa and the Teamsters, 39
Hotel Employees Union, 7, 9
Hutcheson, "Big Bill," 22
Hutcheson case, 98

Idaho, right-to-work law in, 68
Illinois, number of union members in, 9, 10
Industrial unions:
and CIO, 21–28
conflicts within, in collective-bargaining decisions, 60
defined, 14*n*
jurisdictions of, 40
membership policies of, 69–70
Initiation fees, union, 70, 71
Injunction, in labor relations, 95–96, 109, 111–12
International unions, 37, 38, 39, 40
independent, 40
Intraunion coordinating mechanisms, 44–45

Johnson, Lyndon B., 34, 58, 112
Joint Councils, 44, 45
Jones and Laughlin case, 101, 103

Kansas, right-to-work law in, 68
Kennedy, John F., 113
Kennedy, Robert F., 113
Knights of Labor, 15–16, 20, 23
Korean War, 6, 25

Laborers Union, 7
Ladies Garment Workers Union, International, 7, 9, 44, 51, 55
Landrum-Griffin Act, 34, 41, 47, 48, 58, 70, 77, 105, 109, 112–16
evaluation of, 115–16
Laundry Workers Union, 113

Law, in labor relations, 93–116
Lewis, John L., 22, 23, 24, 26, 27, 31, 53, 54
Little Steel companies, 24, 25
Livernash, E. Robert, 69
Local central bodies, 43
Local federations, 43
Local unions, 41–42, 43, 114, 115
  in collective-bargaining decisions, 62–63, 65
  independent, 42
  and trusteeships, 114, 115
  UAW, 64
Locomotive Engineers, Brotherhood of, 41, 69
Loewe Hat Company, 97
Longshoremen's Association, International, 112
Longshoremen's and Warehousemen's Union, International, 28

McClellan Committee, 112–13, 115
McDonald, David J., 24, 55, 60, 61, 71, 79
Machinists Union, 7, 21, 26, 55, 57
Managers, union, 51–55
  salaries of, 52–53
  tenure of, 53–55
Marine Engineers Beneficial Association, jurisdictional claims by, 39–40
Mass-production industries, economic power of workers in, 26–27
Meany, George, 31, 32, 36
Meat Cutters Union, 7, 77
Mechanics' Union of Philadelphia, 13
Mechanics' Union of Trade Associations, 14
Membership in unions:
  and admission policies, 65–70
  compulsory, 65–68, 79–80
  and depression, economic, 83–84, 85, 86
  distribution of, 8–10
  fees and dues for, 70–71
  long-run growth of (1897–1964), 5–6

restrictions on, 68–70
total, 1–2
trends in, 2–3
trends in, as related to labor force trends, 3–5
ultimate authority of, 48–51
voluntary, 80–83
white-collar, 8–9
of women, 9
"Memorial Day incident," in Little Steel strikes, 24
Meyers, Frederic, 79
Milk-Wagon Drivers case, 98
Mine, Mill and Smelter Workers, 28
Mine Workers, United, 6–7, 8, 22, 31, 37, 38, 41, 53, 54
Murray, Philip, 24, 31, 55

NAACP, 68
National Industrial Recovery Act, 100, 101
National Labor Relations Board, 25, 30, 50, 77, 103, 104, 105–107, 109
National Trades' Union, 14
National unions, 37, 38, 39, 40
  independent, 40, 41
  shift of power to, in collective-bargaining decisions, 61–65
  and trusteeships, 114, 115
National War Labor Board (1918), 99
Negroes, and unions, 68, 69
Nepotism, union, 69
New Deal, 2, 98, 99, 100
New England Association of Farmers, Mechanics, and Other Workers, 14
New York City Transit Authority, 49
New York Cloak Joint Board, 44–45
New York State, number of union members in, 9, 10
New York State Crime Commission, 112
NIRA; see National Industrial Recovery Act
NLRB; see National Labor Relations Board

Non-Partisan League, Labor's, 29
Norris-LaGuardia Act, 96, 98, 99–100
North Carolina, number of union members in, 10
North Dakota, number of union members in, 10

Ohio:
    number of union members in, 9, 10
    right-to-work proposal defeated in, 68
Operating Engineers Union, 7

PAC, 29
Painters Union, 40, 44
Panic of 1837, 13, 14
Pennsylvania, number of union members in, 9, 10
Perlman, Selig, 82
Philadelphia:
    Cordwainers case in (1806), 65, 93, 94–95
Picketing, 75
    injunction against, 95, 96
Plumbers Union, 40, 44
Political Action Committee, 29
Priests, American Federation of, 11
Product markets, spread of, 61
Public policy, and unions, 92 ff.
    see also Law, in labor relations

"Raiding" problem, 30
Railway Conductors and Brakemen, Order of, 41
Railway Labor Act, 98–99, 100
Rarick, Donald, 71
Recession, and union growth, 24, 25, 85
Reporting provision, in Landrum-Griffin Act, 114
Republican Political Association of the Workingmen of Philadelphia, 13
Retail Clerks Union, 7, 9, 10, 77
Reuther, Walter, 31, 60, 74–75

Right-to-work laws, 34, 65–66, 67, 68, 109, 110
Roosevelt, Franklin D., 24

Schenley Corporation, 10
Secondary boycott, prohibited by Taft-Hartley Act, 109
Secret-ballot election, union workers', 29, 102–103, 104–105
Service industries, growth of, 4, 64
Sheet Metal Workers Union, 76
Sherman Antitrust Act, 26, 97, 98
Siderographers, International Association of, 37
Sit-down strike, 24
Skilled workers, unionization of, 81–82
Slichter, Sumner H., 69
South Dakota, number of union members in, 10
Stagehands Union (New York City), 68
State federations, 43
Status factor, in unionization, 82–83
Statute law, in labor relations, 93, 98
Steel Workers Organizing Committee, 23, 24
Steelworkers, United, 7, 8, 29, 31, 37, 49, 50, 55, 60, 71, 79, 91
Strike:
    airline (1966), 57
    authorization from union membership, 50
    General Motors (1964), 60
    injunction against, 95, 96, 109
    Little Steel, 24
    national-emergency, injunction as means of coping with, 109, 111–12
    New York City transit (1966), 112
    Pullman (1894), 96
    sit-down, 24
    as union weapon, 75
Supreme Court, U.S., 24, 96, 97, 98, 99, 101, 105, 107
"Sweetheart agreement," 88

SWOC; *see* Steel Workers Organizing Committee

Taft, Robert A., 30, 80
Taft-Hartley Act, 30, 41, 66, 80, 96, 99, 101, 105, 106, 107–12, 114
    Section 14(b) of, 34, 65, 110
Taylor, George W., 59
Taylor, Myron, 23
Teachers, American Federation of, 11
Teamsters Union, 3, 6, 7, 8, 10, 26, 32, 37, 43, 45, 52, 53, 74
    assets of, 78
    bargaining power of, 91
    cost of campaigns organized by, 87
    expelled from AFL-CIO, 32–33, 41, 113
    growth of, 90–91
    income of, 78
    Joint Councils of, 44, 45
    jurisdictional claims by, 39
    locals of, 42
    membership of, 37, 38, 87, 90
Tenure, of union officers, 53–55
Texas, 79, 99
    right-to-work law in, 80
Tobin, Dan, 53
Trade unions; *see* Craft unions
Trades councils, 43–44
Transfer fees, 71
Transport Workers Union (New York City), 49
Truman, Harry S., 112
Trusteeships, union, 114–15
Typographical Union, 50

Unfair labor practices, prohibited by Wagner Act, 102, 103–104
Unfair union practices, prohibited by Taft-Hartley Act, 108–109
Union officers:
    election of, 46–47, 49–50
    salaries of, 52–53
    tenure of, 53–55
Unions:
    beginnings of, 12–14

business, 21, 54, 68, 72–73
Communist-dominated; *see* Communist-dominated unions
craft; *see* Craft unions
decision-making process in; *see* Decision-making, union
economics of organizing, 87–90
elections in; *see* Elections, union
fees and dues, 70–71
finances of, 77–79
frontier, 10–11
future of, 117–18
geographic distribution of, 9–10
growth of, and business cycle, 83–87
history of, 12–34
individual, changes in, 6–7
industrial; *see* Industrial unions
industrial distribution of, 8
institutional needs of, 65–71
international; *see* International unions
and law, 93–116
local; *see* Local unions
management of, 46–71; *see also* managers, union
membership in; *see* Membership in unions
motivation for organizing, 89–90
national; *see* National unions
organizing, economics and motivation of, 87–90
power structure of, 46–48
and public policy, 92 ff.
reasons for joining, 79–83
regionalization of, 45
relations between, 75–77
and shift from goods-producing to service industries, 4
trade; *see* Craft unions
and white-collar workers, 3–4, 82, 83, 91, 117, 118
and women in labor force, increased employment of, 4–5
and women members, 9
Union security, 109–10
Union shop, 67, 69, 79, 80, 109

United States Steel Corporation, 23, 24, 26

Unskilled workers, unionization of, 80–81

Vermont, number of union members in, 10

Vietnam, war in, 6, 8, 86

Voluntarism, 20

Wage guidelines, 91, 92

Wagner Act, 25, 26, 29, 66, 99, 100, 101–107, 108
  operation of, 103–107

Washington, right-to-work proposal defeated in, 68

Webb, Sidney and Beatrice, 51

Welfare and Pension Plans Disclosure Act, 112

White-collar workers, 3–4, 82, 83, 91, 117, 118

Women:
  employment of, 4–5
  in unions, 9

Work permits, 71

Working Men's Party, 13

World War I, 6, 94

World War II, 2, 6, 25, 28, 74, 86, 107

Wyoming, number of union members in, 10

"Yellow-dog" contract, 100

24